PRAISE FOR *GOD, ISRAEL, AND YOU*

I am thankful for the contribution of Michael Onifer on these important questions on Israel, the Church, and God's purposes. I trust that it will be used to give Christians greater understanding and a firm foundation for their stand and action in these momentous days.

—DANIEL JUSTER, TH. D., RESTORATION FROM ZION, TIKKUN INTERNATIONAL

God, Israel, and You is a fantastic book. I read it in two sittings. Michael has given us a very readable, very interesting, and very revealing book about Israel. He has done his homework and filled it with well researched facts that most people have never heard. In fact most likely you never will hear them unless you read this book. I highly recommend it.

—BARRY WISSLER, PRESIDENT, HARVESTNET INTERNATIONAL

Very few people have the experience, intellectual depth, and profundity of heart necessary to write a book like *God, Israel, and You*. Michael Onifer brings us on a journey . . . inviting you to encounter Israel in ways that just may well change your life. I was captured by Israel twenty-five years ago, and have not been able to break free. The magnetism of the people and place, and the story that God has told, is telling, and will tell there, are the center point of all human history. If you have not yet understood that, Michael Onifer and this book will be a faithful and wonderful guide.

—ROBERT STEARNS, FOUNDER & EXECUTIVE DIRECTOR OF EAGLES' WINGS AND
THE INTERNATIONAL DAY OF PRAYER FOR THE PEACE OF JERUSALEM

Most everyone has an opinion on God, and most everyone has an opinion on Israel. That's why *God, Israel, and You* is worthwhile for a broad readership since it tackles the interaction of the two and the various issues resulting from that relationship. In an even-handed, theologically informed, and consistently relevant manner, Onifer and Charles have served up a thoughtful—and thought provoking—piece of work.

—DR. JERRY GILLIS, LEAD PASTOR, THE CHAPEL, GETZVILLE, NEW YORK

The world's largest puzzle has nearly thirty-four thousand pieces. But in real life, Israel is arguably the most complex puzzle of all time. Increasingly our world suffers from diminished attention spans. . . . Few of us have the time and discipline to try and fit the pieces together to get a comprehensive understanding of what's going on at the epicenter. *God, Israel, and You* is a guide to the perplexed. It's a relatively easy read with an artful combination of up-close personal stories, hard facts and scriptural backing. If you want to see the bigger picture of God's redemptive plan for Israel and the nations, this book is for you.

—PASTOR WAYNE HILSDEN, CO-FOUNDER OF KING OF KINGS FAMILY OF

MINISTRIES, JERUSALEM; AND PRESIDENT OF FIRM (FELLOWSHIP OF ISRAEL

RELATED MINISTRIES)

Having sat under Michael Onifer's teaching, I'm surprised by neither the title of this book nor it's heart-stirring content. I have learned much from Michael, and I consider him a good friend. *God, Israel, and You* is both engaging and impactful. Michael Onifer and Joshua Charles use practical, every-day-life stories to explain a variety of layers of Israel's history and context. By the time you finish reading this book, you'll have a deeper love for God, a greater compassion for the people in and around the Holy Land, and an expanded desire to visit Israel.

— JERRY DIRMANN, SR. PASTOR, THE ROCK, ANAHEIM, CA

GOD
ISRAEL
& YOU

THE SCANDALOUS STORY *of a* FAITHFUL GOD

MICHAEL ONIFER
& JOSHUA CHARLES

WND Books

GOD, ISRAEL, AND YOU

Published by WND Books, Washington, D.C. WND Books is a registered trademark of WorldNetDaily.com, Inc. ("WND")
Unless otherwise indicated, Scripture quotations are taken from THE ENGLISH STANDARD VERSION. © 2001 by Crossway Bibles, a division of Good News Publishers.

Also cited: The Holy Bible, King James Version (public domain); Young's Literal Translation (public domain); and the *Holy Bible, New Living Translation.* © *1996, 2004, 2007. Used by permission of Tyndale House Publishers, Inc., Carol Stream, Illinois 60188. All rights reserved.*

Book designed by Mark Karis

WND Books are available at special discounts for bulk purchases. WND Books also publishes books in electronic formats. For more information call (541) 474-1776 or visit www.wndbooks.com.

Paperback ISBN: 978-1-944229-12-2
eBook ISBN: 978-1-944229-13-9

Library of Congress Cataloging-in-Publication Data
Names: Onifer, Michael, author.
Title: God, Israel, and you : the scandalous story of a faithful God :
what the Arab-Israeli conflict can teach us about the knowledge of God /
Michael Onifer and Joshua Charles.
Description: Washington DC : WND Books, 2016.
Includes bibliographical references and index.
Identifiers: LCCN 2015038631| ISBN 9781944229122 (pbk.)
ISBN 9781944229139 (e-book)
Subjects: LCSH: God (Christianity) | Bible--History of Biblical events.
Bible--History of contemporary events. | Arab-Israeli conflict--Religious
aspects--Christianity.
Classification: LCC BT103 .O55 2016 | DDC 231.7/6--dc23
LC record available at http://lccn.loc.gov/2015038631

Printed in the United States of America
16 17 18 19 20 21 EBM 9 8 7 6 5 4 3 2 1

To BISHOP ROBERT STEARNS *whose courageous faith and vision for the next generation prepared the way for this book.*

CONTENTS

FOREWORD

There is perhaps no conflict on earth that has attracted as much attention, fostered such controversy, and aroused such powerful emotions as the Israel-Palestinian conflict. For Christians, this naturally causes a number of questions to arise:

Are the Jewish people just like any other people group in the world?

Is Israel just another nation?

Does the modern state of Israel have any relevance to the church?

Can someone be both pro-Palestinian and pro-Israel, or do you have to pick sides?

If you've ever pondered these questions, then the book you're holding is a trustworthy guide for the perplexed. If you've never asked yourself these questions, it's a Godsend! It is Written by Michael Onifer, a committed Christian who loves the Israelis and the Palestinians, with expert research assistance from Joshua Charles, also a committed Christian who cares for Jew and Arab alike, you can be sure that in the midst of the constant heat surrounding this conflict, this book will be a source of light and illumination.

In the aftermath of the Holocaust, many Christian leaders went through a time of soul searching, recognizing how centuries of European, church-based anti-Semitism had paved the way for the Holocaust. As a result, they began to renounce what is commonly called "replacement theology" or "supersessionism," the idea that the church had replaced or superseded Israel in God's plan of salvation, a theology that opened the door to "Christian" anti-Semitism over the centuries. The rebirth of the modern State of Israel in 1948 further underscored the wrongness of this theology, since it was clear that God still had purposes for the Jewish people and that, even today, He was keeping His ancient prophetic promise to bring them back to the land—their land.

Surely this was a miraculous testimony to God's enduring covenant with Israel and a testament to His faithfulness. Surely this could not be explained in merely natural terms, especially with the surrounding Arab nations poised to wipe out the fledgling state and with this beleaguered nation literally rising out of the ashes of the ovens of Auschwitz. Surely God was with Israel. How else could the Six Day War of 1967 be explained other than as an example of divine intervention?

When I came to faith in Jesus at the age of sixteen in 1971, these were the sentiments expressed by the Christians I met. It was simply taken for granted that the modern State of Israel was a fulfillment of biblical prophecy and that Christians should "stand with Israel." And over the years, although I did not encounter these sentiments universally, I certainly encountered them the vast majority of the time, among believers in both America and the nations.

Today, sadly, these beliefs cannot simply be assumed in evangelical Christian circles, especially among the younger generation of believers. These young people, often passionate for justice, have no living memory of the Holocaust, and unless they have toured Israel, they have little or no idea of the nation's miraculous history. For many of them, Israel is the evil occupier, the ruthless military giant oppressing the poor Palestinians. How could such a nation be a fulfillment of prophecy, and why in the world should Christians stand with the occupier?

With the skill of a storyteller, Onifer takes us back to the biblical texts, connecting the story of modern Israel with the story of ancient Israel in the Bible, beginning with Abraham. Michael also takes us into God's heart, laying out for us His great plan of redemption and explaining why God has preserved His ancient people and now restored them back to their ancestral homeland. And he does so with great care for the Palestinians and without whitewashing the nation of Israel. He also sets the record straight, demonstrating how the Palestinians have embraced a false and destructive narrative, one that ultimately hurts them more than it helps them. And he makes clear that the best path to peace and prosperity for the Palestinians is to embrace the people of Israel rather than try to annihilate them.

Best of all, Michael's writing is filled with hope, and as you read this book, your heart will be filled with hope as well. And together with Joshua, Michael makes sure that every "i" is dotted and every "t" is crossed. You will not be misled as the authors take you on this journey of discovery. The book you now hold in your hands is a Godsend.

I encourage you to allow this book to challenge you and to change you. You will be informed and inspired, and you will learn that by standing with Israel, you can stand with the Palestinians as well.

—MICHAEL L. BROWN, PH.D., AUTHOR OF *OUR HANDS ARE STAINED WITH BLOOD: THE TRAGIC STORY OF THE "CHURCH" AND THE JEWISH PEOPLE*

ACKNOWLEDGMENTS

First and foremost, I want to thank my wife, Asha, for her enduring kindness, patience, and commitment to God and our family. There are several people who have made significant contributions over the years in developing my views regarding Israel: Bishop Robert Stearns, David Nekrutman, Daniel Juster, Linda Olmert, Doug Hershey, Jerry Gillis, and Rabbi Dr. Gerald Meister (of blessed memory). A special thanks goes to our research assistant Catherine Gunsalus as well as to Stephen Clause and David Perkins without whom much of the research and personal interviews would not have been possible. Additionally, I'm deeply appreciative for the excellent work and research done by Jerusalem Institute of Justice. The thoughtful and creative insight of my brother Dana was instrumental in the process of writing this book. I'm also grateful for input from Bill Ostan, Shawn Karns, Justin Rupple, and Luke Crouse. Finally, this book is largely a product of the encouragement and friendship of my coauthor, Joshua Charles.

INTRODUCTION

From a hilltop on the outskirts of Bethlehem, standing on my friend's front porch, you can see the mountains of Jordan to the east. With a slight turn of your head, your eyes pass over the Judean countryside and arrive at Jerusalem neighborhoods. The proximity is unavoidable. The distance between Jerusalem and Bethlehem is shorter than the average commute—one way. The landscape links two countries, one territory, and three religions and creates another inescapable proximity: the peaks and valleys between Israel and Jordan connect the ancient with the present like a wrinkle in time.

The mountains in the distance are home to Mt. Nebo, the summit where Moses saw the Promised Land. This same countryside provided pasture for David's flocks and passage for Abraham as he traveled to Mount Moriah to sacrifice Isaac. What Moses saw from Mount Nebo is modern-day Israel and the West Bank. David's throne was established in Jerusalem, and the temple built by his son Solomon rested on the famed location of Abraham's binding of Isaac. Today that location is the Temple Mount, arguably the most controversial religious site on the planet. The events that happened in millennia past have shaped modern civilization, and today the world's attention is still fixated on this *Promised* Land.

Embraced by the Arab hospitality of legendary lore, I not only enjoy the view from the porch, I've also shared meals, laughter, and tears with my Palestinian hosts. The roles of host and guest have been dissolved by time and exposed the substance of something more enduring and resolute—friendship. While my visits feel more like a homecoming, I recognize, regardless of the depth of relationship, I am a visitor. I also recognize that being a visitor doesn't make me a spectator. Their story is my story; it's your story. Not in some shallow notion of a euphoric universalism, but rather the determined substance of a redemptive history that connects humanity and points to a single, enduring, and eternal hope.

My friend's daughter, in search of work, left her parent's home in Beit Jala for Ramallah, one of the largest cities in the West Bank. On her way to visit friends in Hebron, she stopped in Beit Jala during one of my visits. On the porch, with the mountains in view, we had a conversation that marked my heart as indelibly as the Jordan River marks the terrain and the psyche of Western Civilization. We were discussing her job in Ramallah, and I began asking questions about her goals and her ideal job. At one point she interrupted me: "I see what you're doing. You're asking me about my dreams. I'm a Palestinian; I don't dream."

The injustices suffered by the Palestinian people are a problem. As a Christian I recognize my responsibility to "do to do so: Israel. It's not a defense of Israel for Israel's sake (Ez. 36:22–23) or an attempt to whitewash Israel. It's also not a treatment of the Arab–Israeli conflict. The current conflict is only one of many elements provided in this book so as to give you a wider and more extensive view of the significance of Israel. This book is about finding hope, not only for us, but also for others. It's about recognizing the story where we find a faithful God who is intimately involved with the affairs of mankind; a God who jumps in and gets His hands dirty. From the creation of man out the dust of the earth, to the Incarnation, to the promise of Jesus' return, and with all the wars, famines, and miracles along the way, He's been telling a story.

It's no surprise that movies about comic book superheroes are blockbuster hits. There's good reason for people to flock to visually stunning portrayals of fantasylands hosting grand battles of good and evil. We love epic sagas of good and evil because we're in one. Every nation, tribe, and tongue has a part in God's glorious and scandalous story of redemption.

If there's no room in your heart and mind for a Bible that is both straightforward and mysterious, accessible and infinite, supernatural and practical, or a God who is both holy and wholly involved in the muck and mire of a fallen world, this book probably isn't for you. However, if you can embrace the tension of a paradoxical God and a paradoxical kingdom, then this book could mean the difference between joining God in *His* story, or expecting Him to get on board with yours. Only one leads to true eternal life.

1

JESUS' STORY

For years I didn't own a TV. This was before smartphones, tablets, and video streaming. It was a principled, countercultural decision and one that I have never regretted. Before you think I'm some type of spiritual zealot or just plain weird, you should know that this was during a pseudo-monastic stage of my life. I was single, and ministry was a primary and demanding focus. I was rarely home for much of anything besides sleeping, let alone watching TV. It's also fair to mention that this TV-free lifestyle choice was not made independently and was a ministry-wide commitment.

Today, things are different. Ministry remains a priority, but I've ended the pseudo-monastic stage. I'm happily married with one child and, Lord willing, more on the way. You'll find a flat-screen TV in the living room of our home, along with tablets and smartphones, but we don't have cable or a dish of any kind. I'm still anti-TV and try to do what I can to be *unplugged* and minimize the tidal waves of media capable of consuming my time and attention—not to mention avoiding the inevitable mental atrophy that would result if I were constantly connected. However, from time to time, I enjoy "plugging in" so I can mentally "unplug." At our home we do this through video streaming. My wife and I will find a show we like and go through a season, or seasons, of that show at our own pace. My time on the couch is determined by me and not the hour of the evening or the day of the week.

One Saturday morning my wife and son went out on a playdate and left me home alone for nearly an entire day. It was a rare occurrence, and I decided to plug in to mentally unplug. My actions that Saturday validated the term *zombie vision* as I watched an entire season of a show in which my wife doesn't share my interest. In one sitting I did a whole season!

As with a *Lord of the Rings* or *Star Wars* marathon, you get the whole story at once. There's something about getting the whole story with no interruptions. No commercials, no waiting a week for the next episode or years for the next movie. A friend of mine came to a similar conclusion about how he reads the Bible.

My friend loves the Bible; he's a perpetual learner and an excellent pastor. One day he mentioned that he wanted a Bible without subject headings, numbered chapters and verses, or any of the other encumbering elements provided by most available translations. If he was reading Paul's letter to the Ephesians, he wanted to read it as one letter, as it was intended, with no inter-ruptions. I get his point. And I agree with it. When you read a subtitle before a portion of text, it inevitably influences how you understand it. It creates an expectation, and it often doesn't carry with it the overall context of that particular book of the Bible. Additionally, when one chapter ends, it doesn't mean that a thought is completed or a conclusion has been reached, and unlike a good TV show, it doesn't always leave you at the edge of your seat.

Let's think of books of the Bible as episodes, and the Law, Prophets, Psalms and Proverbs, Gospels, and Epistles as movies. When was the last time you did a "marathon" and got the whole story at once? When was the last time you read through an entire book of the Bible—or read the Bible at all?

A recent LifeWay Research study found that only 45 percent of those who regularly attend church read the Bible more than once a week. Over 40 percent of the people attending are reading their Bibles occasionally—maybe once or twice a month, if at all. In fact, 18 percent of attendees say they never read the Bible.[1] The fact that you're reading this book is evidence that you actually *read* books (according to Pew Research, nearly a quarter of us didn't read a single book in the last year[2]), and it also suggests that, being a reader, you're most likely in the 45 percent who read the Bible more than once a week.

Considering that you're the exception in a post–biblically literate culture,[3] we'll agree that you read your Bible regularly and you're familiar with the history, the people, and the themes of the Bible.

The Bible is essentially one book with two parts. The Old Testament and the New Testament are linked together by hundreds of texts, making the Bible an "incomplete book, of limited value, without both Testaments."[4] This appreciation of the Old Testament is not exclusively Protestant or evangelical for that matter. The Catholic catechism deems the Old Testament "indispensable" and having "permanent value."[5]

If it stands to reason that I should read and understand Paul's letter to the Ephesians it in its entirety, then in order to understand the Bible, it should also be read and understood in its entirety. Jesus came to a people in anticipation of a Messiah, and that anticipation was created by the Old Testament. As we will soon see, Jesus made Himself known by pointing back to the Old Testament.

Before you continue I have a little exercise. First, find a Bible (a real Bible with pages, not the app on your phone). If for some reason, at this moment, you can't get your hands on a Bible, just follow along. For those of you who have a Bible, open it up to the book of Matthew. With the pages facing up and your hand on the spine, lift the book to eye level with the binding between your eyes. Which side is larger, the left or the right? The Old Testament or the New? As you'll see, the Old Testament is substantially larger, to the point that it seems a little lopsided, doesn't it?

In the Bible I use for my regular Scripture reading, the Old Testament is contained in pages 1–957 and the New Testament in pages 961–1241. This means that the Old Testament has 957 pages to the New Testament's 280, making the Old Testament about three-quarters of the Bible! The following charts reveal the volume of content and the representation of different themes in the testaments.[6]

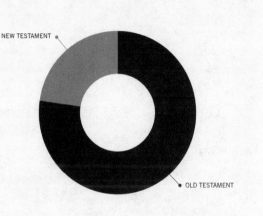

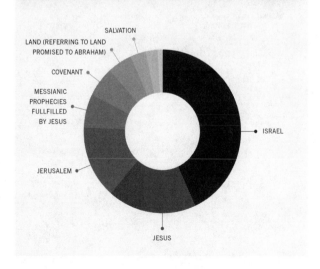

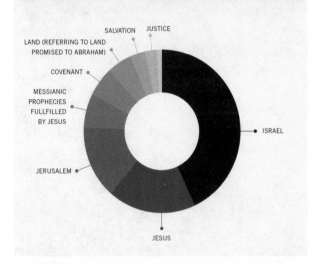

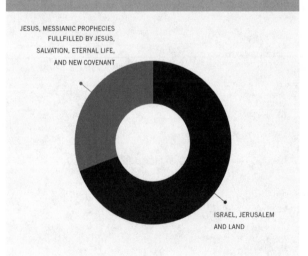

Why the separation between the Old and New Testaments? Just like chapters and verses, it creates a division and adds nothing to the meaning. In this case the interruption has had noticeable consequences. There is a pervasive false dichotomy between what we recognize as the God of the Old Testament and the God of the New Testament. This separation challenges the very nature of God and contradicts how Jesus represented Himself and how the early church represented Jesus.

Did God reinvent Himself in the period between the life of Malachi (the last book of the Old Testament) and the testimony of the Gospels? Four hundred years separate Malachi's days of prophecy and Jesus' birth. There are more than five hundred years between Malachi and David becoming king, more than five hundred years between David's coronation and the birth of Moses, and nearly six hundred years between the birth of Moses and the birth of Abraham. Yet when Jesus spoke about His Father, He spoke of the One who pointed Abraham to the stars (Gen. 15:5), the One Moses saw in the burning bush (Ex. 3:2–4), the One for whom David danced (2 Sam. 6:14), and the One who moved Malachi to foretell of a messenger who would prepare the way of the Lord (Mal. 3:1). The heart of the Father in the garden of Eden, at the binding of Isaac, at the parting of the Red Sea, at the destruction of the first temple, and at the resurrection of Jesus is the same. He is the same yesterday, today, and forever! (Heb. 13:8). Author Daniel Juster, founder of the Messianic Jewish organization Tikkun International, wrote:

> Jesus regularly pointed to Moses and the prophets when speaking of himself, and the Apostles did the same. If we want to know the Jesus of the Bible and the Heavenly Father

he displayed, we need to look cover to cover! We need to expose the false dichotomy between the Old and New Testament and see the majestic and glorious continuity of God's story, "the marvelous, unified, and coherent revelation" of the Bible.[7]

SON OF *JOSEPH*, SON OF *GOD*

Research shows that 90 percent of churchgoers desire to please Jesus in all they do, and 60 percent think about biblical truths on a daily basis.[8] If we're only looking at one-quarter of who Jesus (the Word made flesh) is, how do we know how to please Him, and how much biblical truth do we have at our disposal? There's only one Jesus, you find Him in the Bible, and He's not what we often want or make Him out to be.

The first verse of the first book of the New Testament reads, "The book of the genealogy of Jesus Christ, the son of David, the son of Abraham" (Matt. 1:1). Jesus, the Master, the Savior, the awaited Messiah, is first directly introduced in Scripture with an ethnic and religious identity. The introduction involves a people: His people, His family and their story.[9] That story reaches back more than seventeen hundred years before Jesus' birth. If you really want to know who Jesus is, you have to know something about Abraham and David. You have to know something about the Old Testament. Jesus often referred to Moses and the Prophets (the Old Testament) to provide the foundation for who He was, and the disciples recognized Him because they knew Moses and the Prophets—the first part of the story. Let's look at a few examples:

In the first chapter of John, we have the account of Jesus' call to Philip: The next day Jesus decided to go to Galilee. He found Philip and said to him, "Follow me." Now Philip was from Bethsaida, the city of Andrew and Peter. Philip found Nathanael and said to him, "We have found him of whom *Moses in the Law and also the prophets* wrote, Jesus of Nazareth, the son of Joseph." (John 1:43–45, emphasis added)

Later in the gospel of John, as Jesus' ministry was becoming more popular and controversial, Jesus also pointed to Moses. Look at Jesus' response to the religious leadership of his day: "Do not think that I will accuse you to the Father. There is one who accuses you: Moses, on whom you have set your hope. *For if you believed Moses, you would believe me; for he wrote of me.* But if you do not believe his writings, how will you believe my words?" (John 5:45–47, emphasis added)

After the resurrection Jesus provided one of the clearest affirmations of Moses and the Prophets as He spoke with two disciples traveling on the road to Emmaus. Shortly after, He also appeared to the eleven disciples:

> That very day two of them were going to a village named Emmaus, about seven miles from Jerusalem, and they were talking with each other about all these things that had happened [the crucifixion and the empty tomb]. While they were talking and discussing together, Jesus himself drew near and went with them. But their eyes were kept from recognizing him. . . . And he said to them, "O foolish ones, and slow of heart to believe all that the prophets have spoken! Was it not necessary that the Christ should suffer these things and enter into his glory?" *And beginning with Moses and all the Prophets, he interpreted to them in all the Scriptures the things concerning himself. . . .* And their eyes were opened, and they

recognized him. And he vanished from their sight. . . . And they found the eleven and those who were with them gathered together, saying, "The Lord has risen indeed, and has appeared to Simon!" Then they told what had happened on the road . . . As they were talking about these things, Jesus himself stood among them, and said to them, "Peace to you!" But they were startled and frightened and thought they saw a spirit. And he said to them, "Why are you troubled, and why do doubts arise in your hearts? See my hands and my feet, that it is I myself. Touch me, and see. For a spirit does not have flesh and bones as you see that I have." . . . Then he said to them, "These are my words that I spoke to you while I was still with you, that everything written about me in the *Law of Moses and the Prophets and the Psalms* must be fulfilled." (Luke 24:13–44, emphasis added)

The apostle Paul also used Moses and the Prophets to proclaim Jesus to the Jews of Rome, as was his custom everywhere he went: When they had appointed a day for him, they came to him at his lodging in greater numbers. From morning till evening he expounded to them, testifying to the kingdom of God and trying to convince them about Jesus both from the *Law of Moses and from the Prophets.* (Acts 28:23, emphasis added)

The wise men must have known the story. How else would they know to look for a Jewish King? The Magi, as scholarship has come to recognize them, most likely knew of a promised Jewish King because of Daniel and his influence in Babylon more than seven hundred years before the birth of Christ. The Magi knew enough of Jewish tradition to seek out Jesus, and Scripture itself clearly puts Jesus inside the story of the Jewish people. Philip recognized Jesus as the One of whom Moses and the prophets spoke. Jesus Himself also pointed to Moses and the Prophets. As if this weren't enough, look how Jesus is described by one of the twenty-four elders in the book of Revelation:

> Then I saw in the right hand of him who was seated on the throne a scroll written within and on the back, sealed with seven seals. And I saw a strong angel proclaiming with a loud voice, "Who is worthy to open the scroll and break its seals?" And no one in heaven or on earth or under the earth was able to open the scroll or to look into it, and I began to weep loudly because no one was found worthy to open the scroll or to look into it. And one of the elders said to me, "Weep no more; behold, the *Lion of the tribe of Judah, the Root of David*, has conquered, so that he can open the scroll and its seven seals." (Rev. 5:1–5, emphasis added)

During John's epic glimpse into the eternal, the resurrected Christ is called "the Lion of the tribe of Judah, the Root of David"—same identity, same family, same story from the first book of the New Testament to the last. This Lamb who was slain to ransom the world *is* the Lion of the Tribe of Judah, the Root of David, the son of Abraham! If you want to understand the Bible, if you want to know who Jesus is and how to please Him, if you want explore the depths of the knowledge of God, you need to know something about Jesus' family, the Jewish people, and their nation: Israel.

2

A FAMILY AFFAIR

One year my wife and I celebrated our anniversary at a bed-and-breakfast near Niagara Falls. During our stay we toured some of the famed Niagara-on-the-Lake vineyards. One of our stops was at a place known as the Teaching Winery. In 2000 the Niagara-on-the-lake campus of Niagara College established the Winery and Viticulture Technician program. You'll never guess what they have at the Teaching Winery . . . vineyards! If you're going to learn how to make wine, you'll obviously need grapes, so you should probably know a thing or two about how they grow.

Which brings me to my point: what never ceases to amaze me is that you can go to college to study the Bible, go to divinity school and get a PhD in theology, all without ever stepping foot in Israel, the home of the Bible! Maybe I'm the only one who finds that outrageous, but then again, I'm a little weird because I don't have TV. Bible scholar and teacher Derek Prince said it best: *"You cannot fully understand the Bible, unless you know something about Israel. And if you are confused about Israel, you are confused about the Bible.*"[1] If you have any desire to understand the Bible and its preeminent subject, Jesus, visiting Israel should be a top priority! It should be more than an item on your bucket list. There should be a commitment to make it happen, not just a wishful hope that maybe one day it might happen.

WHO DOES THAT!

One of my favorite places in Israel is the City of David, or "Ir David" as it's called in Hebrew. This archaeological park is absolutely incredible. Everything about it is extraordinary. The story of Eilat Mazar, the archaeologist who insisted that it was the location of King David's palace; Hezekiah's water tunnel (2 Chron. 32:30); the pool of Siloam, where Jesus healed the blind man (John 9:7); the discovery of bullae (clay impressions) bearing names mentioned in the book of Jeremiah (Jer. 38:1–13)—it's all amazing!

During a recent visit the local guide shared a story about his family that embodies the significance of Israel and the Jewish people. This guy has one of the coolest jobs in the world. He does the VIP tours for Ir David, regularly hosting celebrities, athletes, and billionaires, walking them through thirty-eight hundred years of history. Nearly every day he is meeting famous people and guiding them, but he had not yet taken his children on the tour. His daughter let him know that it was time for a family tour. He happily acquiesced.

The last stop on the tour is on a Herodian road dating back to the Second Temple period (the same period of Jesus). The road was recently excavated, and you can literally walk it up to the Temple Mount, just like the Jewish pilgrims did in Jesus' day. There are even holes in the road where Roman soldiers busted through the stone to pull out and slaughter Jews who were hiding beneath the streets during the siege of Jerusalem in AD 70. At the end of the road near the Temple Mount, there is a replica of an inscription that was found near what is popularly known as the Western Wall. This inscription survived the destruction of the temple in the Roman siege. The temple had served as the primary place of worship for the Jewish people before its destruction. During holidays and at the beginning of the Sabbath, a priest would stand at the corner of the elevated plaza where the temple was located and blow a trumpet. As the guide and his daughter approached the inscription replica, she asked what it was.

"Read it," he replied.

Without hesitation, she looked down at the two-thousand-year-old inscription and said, "The place of the trumpeter." His daughter was eleven years old. She's not an expert in ancient Semitic languages, yet she could read a two-thousand-year-old Hebrew inscription! Who does that!

Hebrew is the only ancient language to be successfully revived, going from a dead language used only for liturgical purposes to being spoken by millions of modern-day speakers. This phenomenal resurrection of the Hebrew language is only one accomplishment of a people who have been among the most oppressed in human history and yet the most beneficial to humanity. What may be the most noteworthy quality of the Jewish people is that along with their language, their religious identity, and their customs, they're still here!

I was able to visit Egypt in both the summer of 2014 and 2015. In 2014 we stayed confined to the north, largely in Cairo. We saw a number of amazing and fabled ancient monuments,

most notably the Pyramids of Giza, as well as other pyramids
further south, such as the Step Pyramid of Djoser and the Red
Pyramid of Sneferu. Visiting the Great Pyramid had been a lifelong dream since
I was a young boy. Never in my wildest dreams did I think I
would ever be in a position to see it until I was well into my
fifties or older! From afar, as I saw it for the first time, it looked
almost small. But as we got closer and closer, the absolutely
colossal size of the structure became apparent. The Great
Pyramid is made up of more than two million stone blocks
and stands nearly five hundred feet high. It was beyond awe-
inspiring to imagine how an ancient people who had not even
discovered iron was able to erect such a building.

It then struck me: these pyramids had been around when
Jesus lived briefly in Egypt. Not only that, when Jesus was on
earth, these pyramids were already twenty-six hundred years old,
making them older in relation to Jesus than Jesus is in relation
to us, for a grand total of forty-six hundred years old today.
The mastery of the engineering, the sheer scale of it all, was
simply incomprehensible. Its builders did not have calculators,
computers, or lasers, let alone construction machinery capable
of moving the massive stone blocks with ease.

My trip in the summer of 2015 was equally, if not more,
awe-inspiring. We were able to see a whole series of temples and
monuments that had been on my bucket list ever since I was a
kid falling in love with the Indiana Jones movies: the temple of
Luxor, the Karnak Temple complex (the largest such complex in
the world), the Valleys of the Kings and Queens, Hatshepsut's
Necropolis, Abu Simbel, and more.

Statues in the temple of Luxor dwarfed all those who went

by, and they were made of whole pieces of stone, particularly heavy kinds, like granite.

Karnak was even more impressive. I had always wanted to see its famous "hall of columns." Thousands of years ago, this was the main portion of the temple. The ceilings, which would have been approximately eighty feet high, were painted with the stars of the night sky. The hall itself contained 134 of these massive columns. Each one would require perhaps four to five grown men with their arms fully outstretched to wrap around the circumference of their base. It seemed as if every square inch of space was covered in hieroglyphics, and in a surprising number of places, the colors of the original paint remained, shining forth almost as vibrantly as they had thousands of years ago.

Queen Hatshepsut's mortuary temple, built into the cliffs surrounding Luxor, appeared almost modern in its design, very similar in many ways to the architecture of the 1930s and '40s, particularly the fascist architecture of Italy and Germany of that era. Additionally, the nearby Valleys of the Kings and Queens were surprisingly awe inducing. These were not just holes dug in the ground, but long, deep, intricate, and beautifully designed tombs. Literally everything was covered in hieroglyphics of some kind, and perhaps more than any other place we had seen in Egypt, the original colors, untouched by the sun and fresh air for so long, were as close to their original vivid vibrancy as anything we ever saw.

Abu Simbel was on a different level altogether. One becomes visually aware of the temple upon seeing the four massive, not-so-subtle statues of the great Egyptian pharaoh Ramses II, each nearly seventy feet high. In ancient times, the temple was in Nubia, not Egypt. Nubia had been conquered by the

Egyptians, and Ramses placed this massive temple (built into a cliff by the Nile) along a well-traveled route so that no one would be in doubt that they were entering the realm of a very powerful kingdom. From the silence of the desert, the temple shouts, "DON'T MESS WITH US." The point is further driven home inside, where Ramses is shown deified by two other Egyptian gods, including the sun god Ra, the chief god in the Egyptian pantheon. The walls are full of graphic images of Ramses conquering his enemies, and contain numerous depictions of gratuitous violence. The whole enterprise was intended to induce awe and arouse fear.

And yet, as quickly as the awe of these monuments was aroused, it disappeared. Into its place rushed a wave of somberness, almost sadness. The question that occurred to me was this: what was all of this even for? The gods in whose name these temples were erected? Part of a forgotten and discarded pantheon. The Pharaohs whose names these structures were meant to perpetuate into eternity? They are barely remembered, if remembered at all. All that remains of the Pharaoh who built the Great Pyramid, arguably the most impressive structure ever constructed by man, is a small figurine of dubious quality sitting in an isolated corner of the Egyptian Museum in Cairo. These Pharaohs no doubt accomplished amazing things, but they spent an enormous amount of resources to secure what they believed to be their eternal destiny. And yet, most of them have had their bodies robbed from their own tombs, and the temples and burial chambers they built are crumbling. They wanted their names to echo through eternity, and yet they are hardly known, and nearly everything they built in stone for all time stands in utter ruins. The gods they sought to placate are no longer worshipped. And little of what they themselves did remains in any meaningful form. These impressive structures are the husk of a long-dead religion, a long-fallen empire, a long-since-deflated ego. We admire their famed monoliths for their conquering of space, but the attempt of their builders to conquer time and to create meaning, their ultimate goals, remain forever undone.

This task that had long since lost its grasp on eternal significance haunted me. Inevitably, one is similarly drawn to question the value of one's own life. What is it being spent for? What, to use a phrase, is the point of my puzzle piece?

But this, in turn, led to another line of questioning directed at the metaphorical puzzle itself, going from the particular to the universal: how could a civilization that was easily the most powerful on planet Earth for thousands of years have crumbled into the dust? And its leaders, once literally thought of as gods in the flesh, and its gods, once believed to be the most formidable deities worshipped among men for millennia, are nearly all forgotten? And even more perplexing, how is it possible that such a mighty civilization lies decrepit in the desert sands while that small tribe of Hebrews, whom they once enslaved, not only remains—speaking their same, native tongue and worshipping their same God of old—but flourishes once more in their ancestral homeland? Finally, how is it that the gods of Egypt are but ancient history known to few, while the God of that tribe of slaves is the object of worship of the majority of the billions of human beings on this planet? If a phrase from the Egyptian Book of the Dead were uttered, no one beyond a select few in the halls of a miniscule number of universities would recognize it. And yet, the ancient worship cry of that tribe of slaves, "Hallelujah," is instantly recognizable the world over, even by those who do not worship the God to whom it is directed. If any of the liturgy conducted by the pagan priests of Ozymandias were read aloud today, even in the native tongue of their hearers, no one would understand it. And yet, the holy book of that backward, feisty tribe of Jews not only continues to be read, but even in this age of widespread secularism, remains the best-selling book of all time, a source of inspiration, encouragement, challenge, and salvation to billions.

How on earth is any of this possible? Most of us would conclude that those with the greater power, the greater wealth, the greater buildings, the greater military powers, and the greater resources would stand supreme in the estimation of the world—that it would be *their* religion that was most widespread, *their* culture that would reign supreme, *their* sacred books and rituals that would fill the souls of the world, *their* language that would remain alive and well. And yet, history shows that exactly the opposite has happened as far as the mighty Egyptians and their feeble slaves are concerned. Today, Egyptians do not even speak their native tongue, but that of the Arabian Peninsula. And yet the Jewish people continue to speak theirs, after more than three millennia.

Not only are the language and culture alive, they've had a profound impact on mankind and Western civilization in particular. Consider the words of John Adams regarding Jewish influence, "I will insist that the Hebrews have done more to civilize men than any other nation. If I were an atheist, and believed in blind eternal fate, I should still believe that fate had ordained the Jews to be the most essential instrument for civilizing the nations. If I were an atheist of the other sect, who believe or pretend to believe that all is ordered by chance, I should believe that chance had ordered the Jews to preserve and propagate to all mankind the doctrine of a supreme, intelligent, wise, almighty sovereign of the universe, which I believe to be the great essential principle of all morality, and consequently of all civilization."[2] And all of this in the midst of being the most persecuted people in world history: pogroms, inquisitions, crusades, vendettas, and holocausts have not stunted this phenomenon in the slightest.

By all accounts, all logic, intuition, common sense, historical observation, and precedent, this should not be happening. And yet it is. What is going on here? What's different about this tribe? What's their story?

PROMISE: FROM A PERSON TO A PEOPLE

In the previous chapter we considered how Jesus was introduced in the New Testament, how He was recognized through an understanding of the Law and the Prophets, how He was proclaimed by the apostles, and how He was presented to John in Revelation. We also noted that the majority of the Bible's content was generated before Jesus' birth. So, where does the story find its focus before the Incarnation? Will we find symmetry in the New Testament presentation of Jesus and the beginning of this family affair? We'll begin at the beginning, in the very first book of the Bible: Genesis.

The first section of Genesis begins with creation, the Fall, the Flood, and ends with an introduction to a people (the patriarchs) and a promise. Following this introduction, Scripture uses over three-quarters of Genesis to focus on one theme: people and a promise. Creation itself is wrapped up before chapter 2 even ends; the fall of man and the exile from the garden are only another two chapters. Noah and the Flood get five chapters, followed by thirty-eight chapters about God's promise to Abraham and his family!

Abraham was a shepherd who dwelt in tents. You can still find people who, like Abraham, live in tents and move from place to place with their herds. Today, they're called the *Bedouin*. Bedouin culture is as interesting as their relationship with modernity is complicated. In addition to their ability to survive in desert climates, one of the hallmarks of Bedouin culture is their tradition concerning hospitality. You can visit places in Israel to learn about this traditional Bedouin hospitality and the ancient custom of receiving guests. Learning about these ancient desert customs of hospitality reminded me of Abraham in Genesis 18 when he welcomed three visitors and interceded for Sodom (vv. 1–33).

These introductions to Bedouin culture are often part of the trips I lead in Israel, and they're always a highlight for the group. In addition to a presentation, they get an amazing meal, a camel ride through the breathtaking scenery of the desert wilderness, followed by a night spent in a tent. The evenings are full of worship around a bonfire, and on a clear night you can enjoy a captivating view of the stars. Sitting around the fire, outside the tent, again I am reminded of Abraham:

> And [God] brought him outside and said, "Look toward heaven, and number the stars, if you are able to number them." Then he said to him, "So shall your offspring be." And he believed the LORD, and he counted it to him as righteousness. And he said to him, "I am the LORD who brought you out from Ur of the Chaldeans to give you this land to possess." (Gen. 15:5–7)

Notice that God incorporated two elements into His promise to Abraham—*people* and *land*. These elements will find continuity throughout Genesis and the Bible. The concluding verses of Genesis contain the last words of Joseph: "I am about to die, but God will visit you and bring you up out of this land to the land that he swore to Abraham, to Isaac, and to Jacob" (Gen. 50:24). Joseph understood that the promise made with regard to ancestors included a *land* and a *people*. In Genesis 15 we witness how this promise becomes a covenant:[3]

> But he said, "O Lord GOD, how am I to know that I shall possess it?" He said to him, "Bring me a heifer three years old, a female goat three years old, a ram three years old, a turtledove, and a young pigeon." And he brought him all these, cut them in half, and laid each half over against the other. But he did not cut the birds in half. And when birds of prey came down on the carcasses, Abram drove them away.
>
> As the sun was going down, a deep sleep fell on Abram. And behold, dreadful and great darkness fell upon him. Then the LORD said to Abram, "Know for certain that your offspring will be sojourners in a land that is not theirs and will be servants there, and they will be afflicted for four hundred years. But I will bring judgment on the nation that they serve, and afterward they shall come out with great possessions. As for yourself, you shall go to your fathers in peace; you shall be buried in a good old age. And they shall come back here in the fourth generation, for the iniquity of the Amorites is not yet complete."

When the sun had gone down and it was dark, behold, a smoking fire pot and a flaming torch passed between these pieces. On that day the LORD made a covenant with Abram. (vv. 15:8–18)

Contrary to the ancient, two-party practice of making a covenant, in Genesis 15 we find only one party walking through the sacrificial pieces: the "smoking fire pot and flaming torch" was, in fact, the Lord Himself (v. 17). (We find several similar descriptions of the Lord in Scripture, including Exodus 24:17; Ezekiel 1:27–28; and Revelation 1:14–16.) God passed between the pieces alone and "swore by himself" (Heb. 6:13). Abraham was promised descendants and land in a covenant that was both eternal and unconditional.[4] It was not dependent on Abraham's actions or the state of his soul, but on God's promise alone. This covenant was reiterated again to Abraham (Gen. 17:1–8), to Isaac (Gen. 26:3–4), and to Jacob (Gen. 35:11–12), but it finds its origins in God's promise to Abraham in Genesis 12:

"And I will make of you a great nation, and I will bless you and make your name great, so that you will be a blessing. I will bless those who bless you, and him who dishonors you I will curse, and in you all the families of the earth shall be blessed" (vv. 2–3).

Ultimately this Abrahamic covenant was intended to bless the nations of the earth, culminating in humanity's redemption through the Messiah. However, Abraham's descendants and the land he was promised became inseparable from that ultimate purpose. God resolved, through a covenant, that redemption would be inexorably linked to Abraham's descendants and the land God promised him. Not only did it set the avenue of blessing to come, it also created the warning of a curse to any who would oppose these two elements of covenant, the *land* and the *people*. From this point, all of human history can be observed as God's unwavering fidelity to His promise concerning the *people* and the *land*. God's unconditional and eternal promise to Abraham embodies His character, establishing a covenant of pure and total grace. Once this "decision" is made,[5] scripture never deviates from it, and human history is powerless to escape it. Everything comes back to this unconditional and eternal promise, and the Abrahamic covenant provides the foundation for all the following covenants.[6] The patriarchs (Abraham, Isaac, and Jacob) set the stage for the Mosaic covenant at Sinai. The one cannot be fully understood without the other. Furthermore, the Abrahamic and Mosaic covenants "are foundational for all future revelation, for God's character and Law are revealed in them."[7] From cover to cover, the Bible is a story about Israel (land) and the Jews (people), and culminates in the person of "Jesus Christ, the son of David, the son of Abraham" (Matt. 1:1). This is a family affair.

Major events and spans of time are covered in the first quarter of Genesis; most of it is concerned with one theme: covenant. God reveals Himself as a covenant-making and a covenant-keeping God, and it is in this context that Genesis zeroes in on one man and his descendants. Our introduction to the knowledge of God thus begins with covenant.

A vital distinction needs to be made between the covenant made with Israel at Sinai (Mosaic) and the covenant made with Abraham. The covenant with Abraham is an eternal and unconditional covenant; the Mosaic covenant is very different in that it is a conditional and a temporary administration of the Abrahamic covenant. Both covenants find their ultimate fulfillment and validation in the new covenant, and all of them are made directly with Israel, for to them belong "the covenants of promise" (Eph. 2:12).

Before we take a closer look at the differences between the Mosaic and Abrahamic covenants, we need to consider an important aspect of the *author's* (God's) perspective: how God relates to time. From our vantage point we see these covenants happening in a linear and cumulative fashion because, for us, time is linear. For God, that's not the case. God is outside of time and exists in all time because all time exists in Him! It's not that God is some kind of time traveler who can just bounce around from one time period to another. Rather, God relates to eternity all at once and has no boundaries concerning time and space. Past, present, and future have no meaning for Him as they do for us.

Thinking in a linear fashion, you and I look at the fourteen generations that separate the Abrahamic covenant and the new covenant and conclude that one replaces the other, that the "new" replaces the "old." From God's perspective they coexist in time. For God, the Last Supper and Sinai are two parts of an *eternal, perpetual* present tense.[8]

The only reason God could make an unconditional promise to Abraham, the reason He could be faithful to that promise and deliver the Hebrews from Egypt, and the reason He could make a promise to David was because He saw the nail-pierced hands of Jesus, the Lamb that was slain *from the foundations of the earth*, He who is from *ancient of days* and *has no beginning and no end* (Rev. 1:8)! With this consideration in mind, we'll return to the "temporary administration" of the Mosaic covenant and the eternal and unconditional qualities of the Abrahamic covenant.

Let's pretend that all of humanity is represented by your neighborhood, and you're having people over to watch a movie. The audience represents humanity; your flat screen is human history, the canvas for the movie; and the DVD represents the Abrahamic covenant—that is, God's full plan for salvation. This movie was created in 4K UHD with the highest quality digital sound distinguishable to the human ear. Finally, the DVD player represents the "administration" of the covenant. By the way, you don't have one! Still with me? Let's review:

the audience = humanity

the flat screen = human history

the DVD = God's plan for salvation (Abrahamic covenant)

the DVD player = administration of covenant

Lucky for you, two of your neighbors have a DVD player you can use. The first neighbor to show up is Moshe. He brings some of his family and his DVD player (Mosaic covenant). Moshe's DVD player works, and the movie can be understood, everything can be seen and heard, and the objective (the knowledge of God) can basically be achieved (see Gal. 3:8). However, Moshe's DVD player can't handle 4K UHD or all the elements of the sound quality. Therefore, much of what's there is not fully appreciated and, at this point, you're only watching it with Moshe and his family (see Eph. 2:12). Eventually some of Moshe's family decide to leave and you run out of popcorn, as well. Thankfully, your other neighbor, Jesús (who happens to be Moshe's cousin) saves the day when he comes with more popcorn and a 4K UHD DVD player (new covenant)! Now you're getting everything that was originally intended with both the picture and the sound. After Jesús shows up, the whole neighborhood (humanity) starts to fill your living room because Moshe's family let everyone know the DVD (Abrahamic covenant) was still playing and gave them directions to your house. Time passes. But before too long—and most important, before the movie is over—Moshe's family comes back to finish the movie. To top it all off, Jesús is serving bottomless bowls of popcorn, and he's going to leave the 4K UHD DVD player . . . forever!

Embodied in the Abrahamic covenant you find God's promise concerning *land* and *people*. "I will make of you a great nation, and I will bless you and make your name great, so that you will be a blessing. I will bless those who bless you, and him who dishonors you I will curse, and in you all the families of the earth shall be blessed" (Gen. 12:2–3). This promise finds its ultimate fulfillment in Jesus, but not its only fulfillment. Prophetic texts often have measures of fulfillment or layers of meaning while maintaining a preeminent purpose and actualization. Abraham's people, the Jews, have been a blessing to the nations in a manner that is uncontested and unprecedented in human history. Mark Twain said this about the Jewish people:

> If the statistics are right, the Jews constitute but one per cent of the human race. It suggests a nebulous dim puff of stardust lost in the blaze of the Milky Way. Properly the Jew ought hardly to be heard of; but he is heard of, has always been heard of. He is as prominent on the planet as any other people, and his commercial importance is extravagantly out of proportion to the smallness of his bulk. His contributions to the world's list of great names in literature, science, art, music, finance, medicine, and abstruse learning are also away out of proportion to the weakness of his numbers. He has made a marvelous fight in this world, in all the ages;

and has done it with his hands tied behind him. He could be vain of himself, and be excused for it. The Egyptian, the Babylonian, and the Persian rose, filled the planet with sound and splendor, then faded to dream-stuff and passed away; the Greek and the Roman followed, and made a vast noise, and they are gone; other peoples have sprung up and held their torch high for a time, but it burned out, and they sit in twilight now, or have vanished. The Jew saw them all, beat them all, and is now what he always was, exhibiting no decadence, no infirmities of age, no weakening of his parts, no slowing of his energies, no dulling of his alert and aggressive mind. All things are mortal but the Jew; all other forces pass, but he remains. What is the secret of his immortality?[9]

The statistics show that the Jewish population is even less than Twain imagined: only 0.3 percent of the world's population! However, they account for over 25 percent of recent notable intellectual accomplishments and 26 percent of Nobel Prizes.[10] Furthermore, Jewish contributions to medical science are responsible for saving the lives of an estimated 2.8 billion people![11]

Israel is one of the fastest and most effective humanitarian aid forces on the planet. Its response to natural and man-made disasters surpasses most nations, and certainly any nation of similar size. Israel had the first field hospital operating in Haiti after the 2010 earthquake. It also responded to the 2004 tsunami in Indonesia, Hurricane Katrina in 2005, and the 2011 earthquake in Japan.[12] More recently, this tiny country sent more than 250 doctors and rescue personnel to Nepal with ongoing efforts to construct transitional housing for people left homeless by the 2015 disaster.[13]

It was Israeli innovation in communication and computer technologies that gave us voicemail, instant messaging, and the Centrino chip.[14] The contribution of this "nebulous dim puff of star-dust" affects our quality of life on a daily basis. For Americans particularly, the *blessings* of the Jewish people are woven into the very soul of our nation. The words inscribed on the Statue of Liberty—"Give me your tired, your poor, / Your huddled masses yearning to breathe free, / The wretched refuse of your teeming shore. / Send these, the homeless, tempest-tossed to me, / I lift my lamp beside the golden door!"—were written by poet Emma Lazarus, a Jew. And Jewish songwriter Irving Berlin wrote "God Bless America." (See appendix 3 for additional contributions.)

In his well-written and thought-provoking book *The Gift of the Jews: How a Tribe of Desert Nomads Changed the Way Everyone Thinks and Feels*, Thomas Cahill attributes far more than intellectual accomplishment:

> The Jews started it all—and by "it" I mean so many of the things we care about, the underlying values that make all of us, Jew and gentile, believer and atheist, tick . . . By "we" I mean the usual "we" of the late-twentieth-century writing: the people of the Western world, whose peculiar but vital mentality has come to infect every culture on earth . . . For better or for worse, the role of the West in humanity's history is singular. Because of this, the role of the Jews, the inventors of Western culture, is also singular: there is simply no one else remotely like them; theirs is a unique vocation . . . the very idea of *vocation*, of a personal destiny, is a Jewish idea.[15]

Destiny isn't just an idea we get from the Jews; it's something that we, as Christians, share *with* the Jews! When Jesus instituted the new covenant at the Last Supper, He, along with His Jewish disciples, was celebrating the Passover, a Jewish holiday commemorating God's miraculous deliverance from Egypt. If we don't know God's story, we won't understand Jesus. And if we don't understand Passover, we won't understand the Last Supper. When Jesus said, "this cup" (see Luke 22:19–20), He didn't wait for a lull in conversation or disrupt an awkward silence and grab any random cup that was in front of Him. Everyone present knew what "this" cup was. The Passover tradition includes four cups, each representing a promise from God to the Israelites:

THE CUP OF SANCTIFICATION—based on God's statement "I will bring you out from under the burdens of the Egyptians."

THE CUP OF JUDGMENT OR DELIVERANCE—based on God's statement "I will deliver you from slavery to them."

THE CUP OF REDEMPTION—based on God's statement "I will redeem you with an outstretched arm."

THE CUP OF PRAISE OR RESTORATION—based on God's statement "I will take you to be My people, and I will be your God."

It was the third cup, the Cup of Redemption, that Jesus used to institute the Lord's Supper, and He associated that cup with His atoning death, saying, "This cup is the new covenant in my blood, which is poured out for you" (Luke 22:20; cf. 1 Cor. 11:25).[16] It stands to reason that the fourth and final cup is the cup from which Jesus abstained, saying, "Truly, I say to you, I will not drink again of the fruit of the vine until that day when I drink it new in the kingdom of God" (Mark 14:25). Jesus, with the new covenant, provides the eternal administration of the Abrahamic covenant. With the shedding of His blood, He linked the church's identity with Israel and the Jewish people by associating the Passover with the Lord's Supper. By leaving the celebration incomplete until "that day," He married the destiny of the church to Israel. By the time Jesus instituted the new covenant, the descendants of Abraham, Isaac, and Jacob had experienced four hundred years of slavery in Egypt, had been exiled to Babylon at the hands of Nebuchadnezzar, and would soon experience another exile in the worldwide Jewish diaspora that resulted from their expulsion from the land of Israel by the Romans. While some Jewish presence would remain, most of the people would be separated from the land. The first exile lasted fewer than a hundred years, the second would last more than fifteen hundred.

REVIVAL TONGUES AND TONGUES IN REVIVAL

Between 1890 and 1914, while tens of thousands of Arabic speakers were emigrating from Palestine, Egypt, and Syria, seeking freedom from religious persecution and famine, Jews were coming home.[17] There were three major waves of Jewish immigration to what was then Palestine, and they're known as the First, Second, and Third Aliyah. *Aliyah* is a Hebrew word meaning "to ascend or go up." To this day, this term is used when Jewish people immigrate to Israel, and it is also used as a label for immigrants themselves. The First Aliyah took place between 1882 and 1903, the Second between 1904 and 1914, and the Third between

1919 and 1923. The presence of the Jewish people back in the land would dramatically increase the quality of life in the region, and, as we'll see later on, the Jewish people would secure religious freedoms previously unknown to the region. Jewish immigration benefited "the financial and economic system of Palestine" for "Jews and Arabs alike,"[18] alleviating the main factors that drove Arab flight prior to Jewish immigration.

At the same time, between 1882 and 1923, events were unfolding in the church that would eventually touch the nations of the earth. When the elements of God's promise to Abraham, the *land* and the *people*, came together at the turn of the nineteenth century, the correlation with the church was astonishing! From the earliest waves of immigration to the formation of a nation and that nation's struggle to survive, we find corresponding activity in the church that demands our attention. The presence of the Jewish people back in the land not only dramatically increased the quality of life in the region; it brought a *blessing* to the nations.

Eliezer Ben-Yehuda, a Russian Jew, immigrated to Israel in 1881 with an intense devotion to do something that had never been done before: revive a dead language into one spoken by regular people on a daily basis. Hebrew, while not extinct, was a dead language and almost exclusively used for liturgical purposes by religious Jews. Ben-Yehuda endeavored to have the first Hebrew-speaking home and for his son to be the first all-Hebrew-speaking child in modern history. By 1909, Tel Aviv, the first Hebrew-speaking city, was founded on the sand dunes north of the ancient port city of Joppa. In 1922, Hebrew was recognized as the official language of the Jews living in Palestine.

Edward Irving, a Presbyterian minister in London, lectured

on speaking in tongues (*glossolalia*) as early as 1828. By the 1880s and 1890s, there was growing popularity in the Spirit-empowered service of the believer. Spiritual gifts, miracles, signs, and wonders were increasingly recognized as a means of spreading the gospel. Dwight L. Moody, Reuben A. Torrey, A. J. Gordon, A. T. Pierson, and A. B. Simpson were all advocates of the relationship between the believer and the Holy Spirit. Simpson insisted that tongues would be restored to the church for use in the spread of the gospel.[19] In 1885 "the Cambridge Seven" went to join J. Hudson Taylor and the China Inland Mission. C. T. Studd was one of several among the seven who sought the gift of tongues, hoping it would be a shortcut to speaking Mandarin.[20] His efforts were in vain, but little did he know that another nearly extinct language was nearing a revival.

By AD 400, speaking in tongues and other spiritual gifts were rarely experienced in the church, despite their continuity for the first three centuries. Between the 1000s and 1800s there were sporadic representations of tongues, but in the early 1900s, with revivals taking place in Topeka (Kansas), Houston (Texas), and eventually culminating in Los Angeles (California) with the Azusa Street revival, there was an explosion of speaking in tongues and miracles. This was not an exclusively American experience, and revival was sprouting up on nearly every continent on the globe. This revival of tongues paralleled the revival of Hebrew and began the Pentecostal movement, which today is hundreds of millions strong around the world, crossing Protestant and Catholic divides. The beginning of the twentieth century witnessed movements that "would bring Israel and the Church back full cycle to their 1st-century points of departure."[21]

When the *land* and the *people* of covenant came back

together, missionary activity skyrocketed, as did global church growth. This correlation only continued through the history of what would become the state of Israel. On May 14, 1948, Israel declared independence and was invaded the next day by five Arab armies seeking to eradicate the Jews. The secretary general of the Arab League said, "It will be a war of annihilation. It will be a momentous massacre in history that will be talked about like the massacres of the Mongols or the Crusades."[22] No such annihilation took place, and the Israeli War of Independence ended in November 1949. This victory is celebrated in Israel on *Yom Ha'atzmaut*, meaning "Independence Day." Among Palestinians, it is recognized as *Yawm an-Nakba*, meaning "the Day of Catastrophe." In chapter 7 we'll see how "catastrophe" has preeminent significance to the Jewry.

In June 1967, Arab armies suffered another humiliating defeat after initiating yet another attempt to wipe out Israel. The Six-Day War resulted in Israel's capturing of the Golan Heights, the Sinai Peninsula, Judea and Samaria (the "West Bank" of the Jordan River), and the Gaza Strip. By far the most significant victory was Jewish sovereignty over Jerusalem for the first time in more than two thousand years. Ironically, the Six-Day War, named for the literal duration of the war, has had prolonged global consequences.[23]

Interestingly, the events that served to establish a modern Jewish state and Jewish sovereignty of Jerusalem corresponded with revivals of global consequence. The 1940s through the '70s were marked by revival.[24]

The Healing Revival of the '40s and '50s, most significantly associated with Oral Roberts and William Branham, saw dozens of ministries marked by the supernatural and massive evangelism campaigns: Billy Graham, A. A. Allen, Jack Coe, and T. L. Osborn, to name a few. What was taking place in America was not isolated to America. Revival was breaking out in South America, with major revivals in Brazil and Argentina, and the church in China began to move into exponential growth at the same time. The charismatic movement began in the early '60s, and the Jesus movement followed soon thereafter,[25] subsiding in the early '80s. Each focused on the supernatural and spiritual gifts, similar to the Healing Revival of the '40s and '50s. Each revival was marked by a similar desire to see the modern church function in the power experienced by the early church. Coincidentally, the charismatic movement reached the Roman Catholic Church around the same time an Israeli flag began to fly over Jerusalem, and the Jesus movement birthed the Messianic movement with a massive influx of Jewish believers recognizing their Messiah. As we will understand in greater depth in chapter 7, Israel and the church were coming "full cycle."

While Jewish immigrants were casting lots on a sand dune north of the ancient port city of Joffa, and establishing the first Hebrew-speaking city (Tel-Aviv),[26] the Azusa Street revival was at its peak, and modern Pentecostalism was born. While I personally agree that spiritual gifts should operate in the contemporary church, I am not endeavoring to make a theological statement with respect to spiritual gifts, such as speaking in tongues and healing, or to endorse Pentecostal doctrine. I'm simply making an observation. You can make up your own mind about the historical coincidence of the revival of Hebrew as a modern language and tongues as a spiritual gift. However, the real challenge here and the question you should be asking is, *how can war and revival go hand and hand in God's story?*

3

WHOSE STORY ARE YOU IN?

During a weekend of ministry in Southern California, I visited with friends who attend one of the largest churches in America, Saddleback Church. At that time Saddleback was doing a series on dieting, and my hosts proudly gave me a copy of *The Daniel Plan*. This was not your run-of-the-mill Christian dieting book! It had a level of professionalism and expertise you would expect from a megachurch with a senior pastor whose book, *The Purpose Driven Life*, sold more than 30 million copies. And the book was endorsed by none other than Dr. Oz! My first reaction (and perhaps yours, as well) to this book? Trendy and commercial. That's it.

Regardless of the common sense and godly merit to *The Daniel Plan*, I evaluated the situation through *my* story. *My* experience inevitably influenced how I *thought* and *felt* about the book. My earliest memories of church were in a Roman Catholic setting. As I reached adulthood, my faith took on an evangelical expression. My fondest memories of church come from a small house church that had an old-school Pentecostal feel to it. Throughout my life as a committed Christian, the services I normally attend rarely have more than a thousand people. Saddleback has twenty thousand. I've also never dieted, I've never been overweight, I rarely meet a meal I don't enjoy, and I usually have room for dessert (a fact that often results in being despised by those who don't share my metabolism). I don't relate to the megachurch experience or dieting; they're not a part of *my* story.

Furthermore, there's something about the success and influence of Saddleback that make some people a little suspicious. Rick Warren is one of the most significant spiritual leaders in the world. When he tweets, about four million people see it, and he was also chosen to give President Obama's inaugural invocation. If I'm really going to understand something about Saddleback, I should know something about the founder and senior pastor, Rick Warren. I should look at it through *his* story, not mine. The Daniel Plan, a faith-based, step-by-step wellness program to help people achieve and sustain long-term health,[1] fits comfortably and effectively in his philosophy of ministry: teaching habits of faith. In Charles Duhigg's book, *The Power of Habit*, Pastor Rick explained, "We've thought long and hard about habitualizing faith, breaking it down into pieces. If you try to scare people into following Christ's example, it's not going to work for too long. The only way you get people to take responsibility for their spiritual maturity is to teach them habits of faith."[2] With that little bit of context, my approach to the Daniel Plan became totally different. How I *thought* and *felt* about it changed. The Daniel Plan has deep spiritual truths that intersect with a universal and essential human habit. Eating is an obvious component of our natural lives, and what the Daniel Plan teaches us is that it's also a part of our spiritual lives. The connection between the spiritual and the natural is imperative.

Stories move our hearts and often govern them, as well. Given the opportunity, stories can pull our minds with little, if any, resistance. This persuasive and often intoxicating power of a story plays an important part in how we understand our world and how we *think* and *feel* about almost everything. The question is, whose story are you in?

Instead of understanding the Daniel Plan through the story of Pastor Rick Warren, I attempted to understand it through my own. I didn't filter, or even consider, my personal bias. I tried to understand a *part* without the benefit of being familiar with the *whole*. I started from the perspective of the individual with no context. This error is all too human but not at all Christian. In fact, it is directly contrary to a biblical view of the world.

Judaism, the progenitor of Christianity, has a narrative and a way of understanding the world that is different from all other religions: it begins with the universal, arrives at the individual, and then returns to the universal.[3] Christianity, along with its sacred texts, shares this narrative with Judaism. The universal (the big picture) is a prerequisite to the individual, and not the other way around! The more I understand the universal— the Creator, His will, His emotions, His desires, and His commands—the more I understand myself and the world in which I live. I need to have a basic understanding of the whole in order to understand the parts. I need to know the *Author* if I want to understand the *story*.

There is a big picture and an ultimate intention that serve as a metanarrative, and all the stories or sub-narratives are within the metanarrative. A metanarrative is the whole, and sub-narratives are the parts. God loves *His story* (metanarrative), and His story includes your story (sub-narrative). His *whole* includes your *part*; and if you want to know where you fit, you need to understand the big picture.

BIG PICTURE PUZZLE PIECES

Let's take Jesus' advice and approach this as a child (Matt. 18:3). My nephew is a puzzle junkie. He loves puzzles and is regularly increasing the number of pieces he's able to deal with. At the time of this writing, he's four, and a good puzzle is one of the few things that will hold his attention for a long period of time (besides "zombie vision"). It's heartwarming to see him at the kitchen table, hovered over the scattered pieces, and working his way to completion. What's fascinating is how he relates to the completed image during the process of putting it together. The more frequently he refers to the final image, the faster he puts the puzzle together.

Consider the *pieces of the puzzle* as personal perspectives or sub-narratives and the *completed puzzle* as the "big picture" or the metanarrative. The individual pieces do little, if anything, to help us understand the grand design, but they provide enough to begin joining pieces together. A puzzle can be completed without the benefit of knowing the end result. It may be a painstaking and tedious endeavor, but it can be done.

The puzzle of theology cannot be completed if we maintain a singular focus on our piece of the puzzle. We can't start with ourselves and work our way out. Without the metanarrative the pieces immediately connected to our piece only provide a section of the puzzle, an indication of the object of focus, but the big picture, the ultimate intention, remains obscure. That obscurity provides sufficient ambiguity to make what we want of the pieces we have. Personal narrative and perspective are relevant, but they're not sufficient in and of themselves. When we begin with our piece, our narrative, and set out to understand the metanarrative without the boundary or restriction provided by the universal big picture, the results can be catastrophic. Modern Hebrew has a word for such a catastrophe. The word, which we will revisit in chapter 7, is *shoah*.

My four-year-old nephew is up to 150 pieces with his puzzles. However, what we're dealing with is one puzzle, one story, with more than four thousand years of pieces, and the completed image includes all humanity—past, present, and future. This is where the puzzle analogy itself goes to pieces. God's story isn't one that can be absolutely and authoritatively understood—no one can say with certainty what the final picture looks like in exact detail except God Himself. God's unfathomable patience and mercy leave ample room for us to fit a few pieces together and start working toward our own, imagined, false picture—our own image, and not *the* big picture. Nonetheless, we can know enough to head in the right direction. A. W. Tozer, a twentieth-century Christian mystic, said it this way in his deeply insightful and prophetic book *Knowledge of the Holy*:

> Yet if we would know God and for other's sake tell what we know, we must try to speak of His love. All Christians have tried, but none has ever done it very well. I can no more do justice to that awesome and wonder-filled theme than a child can grasp a star. Still, by reaching toward the star the child may call attention to it and even indicate the direction one

must look to see it. So, as I stretch my heart toward the high, shining love of God someone who has not before known about it may be encouraged to look up and have hope.[4]

Holocaust survivor, writer, professor, political activist, and Nobel laureate Elie Wiesel was onto something when he said, "God created man because He loves stories."[5] I think we love stories because God loves them. Ultimately the death-conquering love of God and the hope therein is the big picture, the finished puzzle: eternal life, the knowledge of God. So, how about another story?

CHRONOLOGICAL PROXIMITY

From 1754 to 1763, France and Great Britain were engaged in the Seven Years' War. The North American theater of the Seven Years' War is commonly known as the French and Indian War and was fought between British America and New France, with both sides aided by Native American allies. In July 1755, General Edward Braddock set out from Fort Cumberland with British forces on a campaign to take control of Fort Duquesne and Fort Niagara and secure the Ohio territory. On July 9, Braddock's forces suffered one of the most devastating defeats in British colonial history at the Battle of Monongahela.[6] Of the approximately 1,300 men Braddock led into battle, 456 were killed and 422 were wounded. Commissioned officers were prime targets and suffered greatly: out of 86 officers, 26 were killed and 37 wounded.[7]

Native Americans fighting with New France often employed extremely violent fear tactics to demoralize their enemies. They were famous for nailing the scalps of the slain to trees.[8] The

British advance guard, overcome by panic and heavy fire from the enemy, collided with the main body of Braddock's forces.[9] After hours of intense combat, Braddock himself was shot,[10] and the British forces began to withdraw to the Monongahela River. There they were met by Native American fighters with axes and scalping knives, and the British forces began to break ranks and run, fearing a slaughter at the hands of the Native Americans. One of the surviving officers managed to form a rear guard and disengage, leaving piles of dead bodies behind, which were scalped and looted by the Native Americans.[11]

A few days after overseeing Braddock's burial, the surviving officer wrote a letter to his brother, ensuring him that he had survived the battle:

> As I have heard since my arrival at this place, a circumstantial acct of my death and dying speech, I take this early opportunity of contradicting both, and of assuring you that I [am] of the living by the miraculous care of Providence, that protected me beyond all human expectation; I had 4 bullets through my coat, and two horses shot under and yet escaped unhurt.
>
> We have been most scandalously beaten by a trifling body of men.[12]

The letter was written to John Augustine Washington by his twenty-three-year-old brother, Colonel George Washington.

Undoubtedly there is a spectrum of responses to this story. It smacks of buzzwords that surround the debate on American *exceptionalism* and modern Israel's very existence: "colonialism" and "imperialism." What makes it so interesting, however, is that it is simultaneously chronologically close enough to be scrutinized, and distant enough to be romanticized. Regardless of your patriotism, or lack thereof, this story has an Old World allure to it. The quality of the sources are strong, and the historical accounts of the battle verify the events. We benefit in that regard due to the chronological proximity of the events. We see a bigger picture, with people, places, events, relationships, politics and, in this case, the miraculous. According to Washington's personal account of four bullets through his coat and two horses shot from under him, as well as the devastating number of dead and wounded, it's easy to see how he credits his survival to *Providence*. In this case, our appreciation of the miraculous is not without substantiated historic record.

What if we lost the benefit of chronological proximity? What happens when we don't have all the evidence and, instead of a tapestry, we have only a few sturdy threads or a few pieces of the puzzle? What happens when we examine events in antiquity? One could anticipate an interesting correlation between the lack of historical and archaeological verification and the increased sense of romanticism. It would also be safe to assume, without all the evidence, that the affairs of nations, armies, politicians, soldiers, and civilians were just as complex and human as they are today. Just as human and real as they were at the Battle of Monongahela in 1755. And Providence is just as miraculous.

One of the prophecies in the Bible concerns Cyrus II, a Persian king who reigned from 539 to 530 BC. The prophet Isaiah wrote of Cyrus by name and of his role in returning the exiled Hebrews to their homeland more than one hundred years before Cyrus was born (Isa. 45:1–6). In accordance with the prophecy, King Cyrus (better known as Cyrus the Great) came to power in 539 BC, established the Persian Empire, and sent the Israelites back to Jerusalem with the instruments of the Temple—just as Isaiah had prophesied! This event is historic fact, upheld by scholarship and archaeology, but we know little of the complexities and humanity that were undoubtedly woven into the chain of events. I'm confident that if we knew the details, if we had a bigger picture instead of just a few pieces, it would be as intriguing as the George Washington story and material for Hollywood's next Bible-based blockbuster.

Cyrus II is one of hundreds of biblical examples and one of countless historical examples of how God's redemptive purposes are woven into history and executed through fallen humanity—real people. God uses nations, rulers, shepherds, donkeys, angels, demons, celestial bodies, earthquakes, floods, and even fire from heaven—whatever He wants! When our consideration of biblical events passes the threshold of superficial recognition, when we acknowledge that events happened and they are both historic and miraculous, we can appreciate that nothing happens in a vacuum. There is always a bigger picture, a backstory, an intricate arrangement of relationships and events. In this orchestration of pieces, we encounter the awe and mystery of God's unwavering commitment to fulfill His Word and His ability to use anything and anyone. We find that "all things work together for good" (Rom. 8:28).

God plays in the dirt; He jumps in and gets His hands dirty in the affairs of humanity. Not only has God always been involved, but humanity unceasingly demonstrates little change in character. To echo King Solomon, "there is nothing new under the sun" (Eccl. 1:9). God uses whatever and whomever He wants to accomplish His purposes, and He executes His plans through real people, places, and events. George Washington and Cyrus the Great were both remarkable figures in history. They were both human, both flawed, and each of their lives contained some elements of conspiracy or scandal. And the closer these figures are to us, the easier it is to find the incriminating evidence that joins them to a broken human race. However, the examination of these individuals, a magnified few of one piece, doesn't give you the big picture. Proximity to an object, or an up-close, magnified view of one piece of the puzzle, affects how we see the big picture and how easily we put the puzzle together.

To understand the story of Cyrus, we have to understand the story of Israel. To understand the story of Israel, we have to understand the story of the Bible. When reading the Bible, we are forced to recognize that imperfect men and women, even downright godless men and women—anything or anyone, visible or invisible—is a part of the story, and they are all at the service of the *Author* (see Rev. 4:11). To say it another way (modifying the quote from Derek Prince in chapter 2): if we are confused about Israel, we will be confused about the Bible, and if we're confused about the Bible, we won't recognize God, and we certainly won't understand a God who gets His hands dirty.

It's hard to find a biblical hero without some scandal. Noah became a drunk. Abraham had a contentious household, to put it mildly. Judah slept with his daughter-in-law, mistaking her for a prostitute. Moses was guilty of murder and, for other reasons, was kept from entering the Promised Land. David's sin of adultery was followed by murder. And that's the short list! And these are patriarchs and heroes of faith! What about the Gentiles in the Bible? Take your pick of heroes or villains; their imperfect lives are perfectly arranged in God's story: Pharaoh, Jethro, Balaam, Ruth, Haman, Rahab, Naaman, Nebuchadnezzar,

Cyrus, the Magi, Pontius Pilate, Cornelius, and so on.

The power of story, the context, the individual perspective—both God's and our own, how *we* view God's dealings with humanity—influence how we *think* and *feel* about everything, especially Israel. God's story is a *dirty* one, and to understand our own story, you have to start with His—not the other way around. Later on we'll further examine how a *parts to the whole*, instead of a *whole to the parts*, way of processing is symptomatic in the way Christians deal with modern-day Israel. For now, let's return to the predicament of an up-close, magnified view.

Imagine your hometown is Nazareth and you're alive during Jesus' earthly ministry. You know Jesus, the son of Joseph the carpenter. Like everyone else in the small village of Nazareth, you also know of the scandal surrounding Jesus: the timing of His birth, the marriage of Joseph and Mary, and the speculation that Joseph is not the real father. You're in the local synagogue on the Sabbath, and Jesus is approaching the scroll of Isaiah. Your evaluation of Him is immediate and subconscious. You've known Him for years; you know His family; you live in the same small village—He's connected to your piece of the puzzle; He's up close and magnified.

Jesus has done this before, but today is different. Very different. Jesus has recently begun teaching throughout the region of Galilee, and everyone is talking about Him. Jesus begins to read: "The Spirit of the Lord is upon me, because he has anointed me to proclaim good news to the poor. He has sent me to proclaim liberty to the captives and recovering of sight to the blind, to set at liberty those who are oppressed, to proclaim the year of the Lord's favor." Every eye is fixed on Jesus as He rolls up the scroll and sits down. Then He speaks again: "Today this Scripture has been fulfilled in your hearing" (Luke 4:16–21). That's when everyone, including you, starts to freak out! His statements collide with your up-close, magnified view, and the gravity of His words carry the weight of eternity. The question you ask yourself is the same one everyone else is asking: "Isn't this Joseph's son?"

That day in the synagogue, people were presented with a choice, a choice that all of Israel would eventually have to make, and a choice that people are still making today—including you. How do we recognize Him: as the son of Joseph or the Son of God? The paradox for the people who were actually present in that synagogue more than two thousand years ago was this: both were true! Their response would be influenced by their magnified, up-close view of the events and the people involved. Which story would they prioritize: their story or *the* story? Were they going to make their choice, starting with the big picture, working down to their own individual piece, or the other way around? Will you see the son of Joseph through the context of God's story and recognize the Messiah, or will you see the son of Joseph through your story and fail to embrace eternal life? Philip the disciple embraced the tension of the paradox when he came to Nathaniel and said, "We have found him of whom Moses in the Law and also the prophets wrote, Jesus of Nazareth, the son of Joseph" (John 1:45).

In one way we are very similar to the people sitting in that synagogue. In fact, we might have a greater association with the Pharisees than the fishermen he called to be disciples! If we have a biblical worldview, if church is more than a place we go on Sunday out of obligation, if we take seriously our religion (in the most positive sense of the word), we're modern-day Pharisees.

The Pharisees had something to say about Jesus because they had a very high view of Scripture and religious tradition. They weren't the religious elite (Sadducees); they were the everyday, spiritually devoted of their time. If we fit the description above, we're the spiritually devoted of our time. Our faith is not just a cultural dynamic; it influences our daily decisions, and we think about the world, the past, present, and future, through the lens of Scripture. Like the Pharisees, we usually have something to say, or at least a concern, about subjects that are relevant to our beliefs. If we take the time to consider it, we probably have just as much tradition and ritual in our lives as they did.

The Pharisees of Jesus' day had roughly two thousand years of history between them and Moses at Sinai. We have roughly the same amount of time between us and Jesus at the Last Supper. The Old Testament is "pointing beyond itself,"[13] and Jesus pointed back to the Old Testament. Jesus is the climax the Old Testament was awaiting; He is the "fulfillment" of the prophecies, and not all of them are fulfilled. Jesus brings a climax to the story but not an end. We are still in the story, and it's not over. Both the Old and New Testaments carry anticipation and point to things yet to be. The people who were in the synagogue with Jesus when He read from Isaiah had to filter two thousand years of tradition as prophecy was being fulfilled before their eyes. You and I are just as human as they were, and just like them, we have two thousand years to filter when prophecy is fulfilled before our eyes. We have our own interpretations of how to worship, how to pray, how to live, and how to discern the fulfillment of prophecy. The Pharisees of Jesus' day had developed expectations of a coming Messiah, and we have expectations about His return. To suggest their nature was any different from ours is adolescent at best and haughty at worst. Jesus met the needs of the Pharisees. The Pharisees (past and present) needed to see their need for Jesus.

Like the Pharisees, we ourselves have thousands of years of traditions and cultural narratives that affect how we expect to see God behave. The Israelites of Jesus' day had generations to cultivate religious tradition, and so has the church. Today, we are up close and personal, not with a man in a synagogue claiming to be the Messiah, but with the presence of a Jewish nation regathered from the nations of the earth and the scriptural implications of that reality. It is the "big picture" of this reality that we turn to next.

4

HATRED THAT PASSES UNDERSTANDING

On November 9, 2010, President Barack Obama was visiting Indonesia. During a press conference with Indonesian president Susilo Bambang Yudhoyono, he was asked about plans for apartment buildings in Jerusalem.[1] At first glance, given the media attention on Israel, this may not seem odd. Additionally, the Arab–Israeli conflict and negotiations regarding a "two-state solution" were on the agenda for Obama's visit. However, if we take a step back and look at the big picture, we can learn something, something that is often overlooked in the copious coverage and criticism of Israel.

Jerusalem is more than fifty-three hundred miles from Jakarta and over fifty-eight hundred miles from Washington, DC. Indonesia has a total landmass that exceeds 1.1 million square miles, and the United States exceeds 3.5 million. According to the US Census Bureau, the United States ended 2014 with a population of 320 million, and Indonesia, the world's largest Muslim nation, had 252 million.[2] Israel's population in 2014 reached 8.2 million, and her total land mass is a whopping 12,632 square miles!

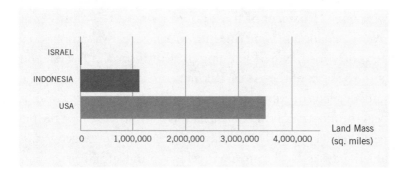

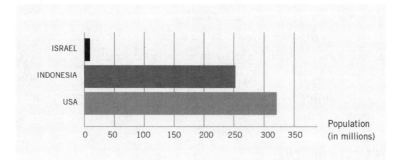

One can't help but wonder why Jerusalem, the capital city of Israel, a tiny sliver of a nation more than five thousand miles away from each of these nations, demands their attention? And not even Jerusalem or Israel as whole, but a few apartment buildings in Jerusalem! What other conflict, past or present, has received such overwhelming attention?

A 2013 BBC World Service Poll generated very interesting findings concerning the perception of Israel in the world.[3] More than twenty-six thousand people from twenty-two nations were asked to rate sixteen nations and the EU. Participants had to decide if each nation's influence in the world was mostly positive or mostly negative. Israel placed fourteenth out of seventeen, with only 21 percent of those polled rating her as mostly positive. The nation placing fifteenth with an approval rating of 19 percent? North Korea! Coming in at thirteenth is Russia, and at the bottom of the list are Pakistan and Iran. Considering the unparalleled contribution of the Jewish people to the world, it begs the question, how could a nation comprised of such people be perceived so poorly? To fully appreciate how outrageous and illogical this is, we'll compare Israel to North Korea, Russia, Iran, and some of Israel's nearby neighbors. The result, in light of this poll, truly passes understanding.

To do this we'll look at how Israel relates to issues currently monopolizing global media and conversation. These topics typically invoke passionate debate and strong opinions: the environment, the LGBT community, women's rights, and religious freedom.

THE ENVIRONMENT

The diversity of Israel's landscape is incredible. You can go skiing in the north on Mount Hermon, and scuba diving in the south in the Gulf of Aqaba. Between those northern and southern points you'll find just about every type of topography: forests, agricultural plains, mountain ranges, beaches, and deserts. You can drive from Mount Hermon to the Gulf of Aqaba in about eight hours, and along the way you'll pass national parks impressive to history buffs and nature lovers alike. There's a lot packed into this tiny nation! From Tel Megiddo along the Jezreel Valley to the En Gedi spring along the shores of the Dead

Sea, the landscapes are as breathtaking as they are cherished and cared for. Israel is one of the greenest, most eco-friendly nations on the planet.

Israelis recycle more than Americans and Europeans! In fact, the ELA recycling company reported that Israelis recycled 50 percent of the country's plastic bottles in 2011, surpassing Europe's 48 percent and the United States' rate of 29 percent.[4] Israel, as a whole, recycles 25 percent of all waste generated.[5] Egypt, on the other hand, recycles approximately 10 to 15 percent of all waste, and 80 to 88 percent of waste is openly dumped.[6] Jordan comes in at 7 percent.[7]

The Israeli Knesset is the greenest parliamentary building on the planet. In 2015 the Knesset unveiled a 4,650-square-meter solar field that consists of 1,406 photovoltaic panels, which provides 450 kilowatts of energy.[8] But Israeli conservation measures aren't limited to energy. The nation is also at the forefront of water conservation. In March 2014 Israeli prime minister Benjamin Netanyahu visited California and signed an agreement with Governor Jerry Brown that Israel will export Israeli water technology to help California cope with drought.[9] Israel's innovative water conservation, which utilizes desalination, drip irrigation, and greywater treatment, has had a global impact.

LGBT COMMUNITY

Gay rights, specifically marriage, and the exposure of LGBT lifestyles has remained at the forefront of politics and culture, with all indicators suggesting that this will remain a heated issue. The US Supreme Court ruling on same-sex marriage will affect numerous sectors of society, the magnitude of which remains to be seen. Caitlyn Jenner has become an icon of the

LGBT community, and the issue has become intensely polarized. Regardless of where you stand, the fact of the matter is that anyone opposing the "rights" or the agenda of the LGBT community is an object of vehement scorn from the majority of mainstream media outlets.

In America there is an appearance of widespread celebration when entertainers, athletes, or celebrities of any kind publicly acknowledge their homosexuality or actualize their gender identification when it differs from their physiological gender. This same phenomenon can be seen in Europe, where the general sentiment toward the LGBT community and alternative lifestyles is favorable.

The celebrity of Austria's Thomas Neuwirth provides evidence of the European sentiment. Thomas became a European superstar after winning the 2014 Eurovision Song Contest, but you've probably never heard of him. That's because he won as Conchita Wurst, his drag stage persona. In drag and a full beard, Conchita has become an icon for the LGBT community. He performed for the European Parliament and even UN general secretary Ban Ki-moon at the UN's Vienna office.

And yet, while global opinion appears to be in favor of the LGBT community, it is not in favor of Israel. So, one would assume that a nation seen slightly better than North Korea but no better than Russia would have a poor record in regard to its LGBT community. However, that is not the case at all.

More than a decade before the US Supreme Court ruling on same-sex marriage, Israel became the first nation on the continent of Asia to recognize same-sex unions, in 1994. In 1988, consensual gay sex became legal. Laws regarding discrimination based on sexual orientation were enacted in 1992. Tel

Aviv, the cultural center of Israel, hosted its first Pride Parade in 1997, which has since become an annual event. The 2010 parade had an attendance exceeding one hundred thousand. Military service for homosexuals became legal in 2000, a full decade before the US military began to accept openly gay or bisexual individuals for service. In January 2015 Philadelphia mayor Michael Nutter officiated the same-sex marriage of an Israeli diplomat.[10] In virtually every respect Israel is ahead of the United States, and we haven't even begun to look at North Korea, Russia, or Israel's neighbors.

What about gay rights in North Korea and Russia? In an article written on this very question, gay life expert Ramon Johnson took up the issue of the LGBT community in North Korea. He stated, "Homosexuality is not explicitly illegal, but it is shunned by the government as promoting consumerism, classism and promiscuity. Gay North Koreans either live in secrecy or enter heterosexual marriages with little or no understanding of their sexuality."[11] In contrast to North Korea, homosexuality in Iran and Saudi Arabia is punishable by death.[12] Russia decriminalized homosexuality in 1993 but maintains laws against the "propaganda of non-traditional sexual relations among minors."[13]

While Israel has been ahead of the curve with respect to the worldwide trend in favor of LGBT rights, this apparently had little influence on Europe's perception of Israel. The European nations polled in the BBC poll mentioned earlier averaged 7 percent below the global average for rating Israel's influence as positive: 13 percent versus 20 percent. Adding to this conundrum is that conservatives, in America or elsewhere, who maintain traditional views on marriage, sexual orientation, and gender issues are categorically viewed as allies of Israel. Religious conservatives aren't celebrating Israel's position, and apparently 79 percent of people polled see Israel's influence in the world as negative.

WOMEN'S RIGHTS

Simply put, Israel is the best place to be a woman in the Middle East! Women have full rights and access to society and culture on all levels. Israel had a female prime minister from 1969 to 1974 (the fourth woman in the world to hold such an office), and at the time of this writing, there are twenty-eight female members of Knesset out of the 120 seats that comprise Israel's legislative body—a higher percentage than female representation in the 114th US Congress.

What's most admirable about Israel's treatment of women is what they have done in traditional communities to elevate the status of women and maintain traditional values. This can be seen dramatically within the Bedouin and Druze communities.[14] Ben Gurion University in Be'er Sheva, Israel, provides generous scholarships to the Bedouin community, providing the means for women to maintain cultural and religious traditions while pursuing a college education. With an estimated Bedouin population of 250,000 in Israel, there are 350 women enrolled for studies at Ben Gurion University.[15] Magda Mansour, a member of the Israeli Druze community, was the first in her village to get a college degree. Today Magda has a master's in English and speaks about her life in Israel as a woman who is both an ethnic and a religious minority.[16]

In *The Global Gender Gap Report 2014*, Israel outranked all of her neighbors. Israel was sixty-four nations ahead of the next ranking awarded to a bordering nation.[17] Egypt, Israel's neighbor to the West, legally requires women to obey their husbands, as is also the case in the disputed territories of Gaza and the West Bank. To Israel's north, in Syria, as well as in Egypt, Gaza, and the West Bank, abortions are only permitted in order to save a woman's life and are illegal under any other circumstances, including rape and incest.[18]

Honor killings may be the most heinous violation of women's rights in the Islamic world. An honor killing is the murder of an individual by members of their family (most commonly, but not exclusively, a woman murdered by a male relative) for having, or rumored to have had, sex outside of marriage, being the victim of rape, engaging in homosexual acts, and apostasy.[19] Iran, Saudi Arabia, Egypt, Jordan, Syria, Gaza, and the West Bank do *not* outlaw honor killings. In the first ten months of 2014, there were seventeen known cases of honor killings in the Palestinian Territories.[20] According to the UN, the estimated global total of annual honor killings is five thousand, with the probability of that number being as much as four times greater.[21] Several honor killings have even happened in America.[22]

RELIGIOUS FREEDOM

Along with being the best place in the Middle East to be a woman, Israel is the best place to be a religious minority. There are daily reports of brutality against religious minorities, especially Christians, in Asia, Africa, and the Middle East. Rarely, if ever, do such reports come out of Israel! The current religious freedoms experienced in Israel find their origin in the same Judeo-Christian ethic that founded religious freedom in America. Theodor Herzl, the father of Zionism, wasn't religious but was significantly influenced by scripture and Christian theology regarding Israel.[23] "Every man will be as free and undisturbed in his faith or his disbelief as he is in his nationality," he wrote. "And if it should occur that men of other creeds and different nationalities come to live amongst us, we should accord them honorable protection and equality before the law."[24]

Israel's declaration of independence maintained Herzl's ideals of religious freedom,[25] and one of the greatest examples of Israel's commitment to religious freedom is the Temple Mount. Israel's decision to allow Muslim religious oversight to the Temple Mount after capturing the Old City of Jerusalem and the Temple Mount in the Six-Day War is a monumental statement of Israel's fidelity to religious liberties. The following account comes from Israel's minister of defense during the Six-Day War, Moshe Dayan:

> I thought that the first unequivocal decision that had to be made concerned the direction and supervision of the compound of the mosques and the Moslem offices. On the morning of the first Saturday after the war, I visited the El Aksa Mosque and met the Moslem religious personnel responsible for it. I reached the court of the mosque by way of the Western (Wailing) Wall. Access to the Wall had been denied to Jews for the previous nineteen years, and now as we passed it, thousands of Jewish worshipers crowded against its ancient stones in ecstatic celebration. As we continued through the Mograbi Gate above to reach the mosque compound, it was as though we were suddenly cut off from a world filled with joy and had entered a place of sullen silence. The Arab officials who received us outside

the mosque solemnly greeted us, their expression reflecting deep mourning over our victory and fear of what I might do.

Before entering the mosque, I asked the Israeli officers who were with me to take off their shoes and leave their weapons behind them . . . As a consequence of the battle for Jerusalem, their water and electricity had been cut off. I promised that both would be restored within forty-eight hours. I then plunged directly into the main issue. I said that the war was now over and we had to return to normal life. I asked them to resume religious services in the mosque on the following Friday. I said I had no wish and no intention of continuing the practice which the Jordanians had instituted of censoring Friday's sermon before it was broadcast.

I said that Israeli troops would be removed from the site and stationed outside the compound. The Israeli authorities were responsible for overall security, but we would not interfere in the private affairs of the Moslems responsible for their own sanctuaries. These were two Moslem places of worship, and they had the right to operate them themselves. My hosts no doubt knew that on the day we had captured this site, I had given orders that the Israeli flag be removed from the Mosque of the Dome, where it had been hoisted. We had no intention of controlling Moslem holy places or of interfering in their religious life. The one thing we would introduce was freedom of Jewish access to the compound of Haram esh-Sharif without limitation or payment. This compound, as my hosts well knew, was our Temple Mount. Here stood our Temple during ancient times, and it would be inconceivable for Jews not to be able freely to visit this holy place now that Jerusalem was under our rule.[26]

Israel's protection of religious rights for minorities cannot be overstated. The lengths to which Israel has gone is admirable, exemplary, and distinct in the Middle East. Despite Dayan's efforts, the Temple Mount is one of the most tumultuous pieces of real estate on the planet. Under the management of the Jerusalem Muslim Wakf, Jewish access is very controversial. But Jewish access to the Temple Mount is not the only issue; access for all non-Muslims is a challenge and stands in stark contrast to the freedoms Israel maintains.

On multiple occasions I have been harassed on the Temple Mount, and several times (spanning several years) have witnessed children, boys and girls, chanting in Arabic, "We will liberate Palestine with our flesh and our blood." On August 11, 2015, a delegation of US Congressmen experienced what I've been dealing with for years when I visit the Temple Mount. The following are excerpts from the Jerusalem Post coverage of the events:

> "There was an effort to completely suppress not only any expression of religious conviction, but any articulation of historical reality," Rep. Trent Franks (R-Arizona) . . . recounted. . . .
>
> "We walked up there, and were almost immediately approached by several men who started shouting," [Rep. Keith] Rothfus [R-Pennsylvania] said. "We were tracked the entire time we were there and found these individuals surprisingly intolerant and belligerent."
>
> The delegation said the harassment began when they ascended the Mount, and a man yelled at Elizabeth Jenkins— who was wearing a calf-length skirt and a long-sleeved

shirt—that she needed to cover up more. Police were needed to break up the melee and clear the way for the group to continue its visit. . . .

Soon after 15–20 men began to harass the group, interrupting the tour guide, shouting and pointing, and once again police were needed to break up the commotion.

"I wish it was something the world understood more and was more aware of," Franks said. "Even when visiting a historical site there is harassment, because of people who want to rewrite history."[27]

Franks said while he doesn't question Israeli policies on the Temple Mount, he found that "in general, when there is a lack of resolve in protecting religious freedoms, it emboldens those who have no compunction about suppressing it." Rothfus said he "certainly" felt his freedom of expression was violated.

"We weren't doing anything religious," he said. "We were learning the history of the Temple Mount."[28]

Sadly, the Palestinian Territories, Gaza, and the West Bank (Judea and Samaria) exhibit the intolerance of the Muslim Waqf. According to the Palestinian Basic Law, as stipulated in Article 4, Islam is the official religion and "principles of Islamic Shari'a shall be the main source of legislation."[29] That being the case, there's little, if any, judicial protection for non-Muslims and women. In the 1920s, 80 percent of Bethlehem was Christian. Under Palestinian rule it has a Muslim majority.[30] Christians living in the West Bank and Gaza are harassed; places of business have been burned; young Christian girls have been gangraped, kidnapped, and murdered; and even the corpses of

Christians have been mutilated.[31] Christians regularly remain quiet about mistreatment and offenses for fear of arbitrary arrest, torture, and the accusation of cooperating with Israel.[32] When Hamas gained control of the Gaza Strip in 2005, they set fire to the Bible Society's bookstore, the owner was kidnapped, and his body was later found mutilated.[33]

Ironically, Israel is accused of discrimination toward its Arab population, and very little attention is given in the UN, the European Union, or international media concerning Palestinian human rights violations. Israel is commonly regarded as an "apartheid state," a reference to apartheid South Africa. This rhetoric is commonplace and increasingly accepted as fact. Consequently, the concrete sections of Israel's security fence separating Israel from the disputed territories of the West Bank have come to be known as Israel's "apartheid wall." But not only is the accusation of apartheid grossly inaccurate and insulting to black South Africans who suffered under apartheid, if Israel *were* an apartheid state, there would be legal discrimination by a ruling ethnic minority against the ethnic majority. This simply does not exist in Israel! The South African justice, Richard Goldstone, credited with providing the legal basis to overturn apartheid in South Africa, denounces this accusation and acknowledges it as an impediment to negotiations between Israelis and Palestinians.[34] The idea of comparing the laws and demographics of Israel to apartheid South Africa is absurd!

Israel is the only safe haven for religious minorities and the LGBT community in the Middle East, an uncontested regional leader in gender equality, and one of the world's most environmentally friendly nations in the world—and yet she is regarded only a little better than North Korea and worse than Russia in the eyes of the world! This hatred surpasses understanding. It is divorced from natural logic and too widespread to be considered coincidental.

THE ARAB–ISRAELI CONFLICT

One potent source of international discontent is the Arab–Israeli conflict and the events surrounding Jewish immigration to Israel and the reestablishment of a Jewish homeland. Without question the ongoing and unresolved issues between Israel, the Palestinians, and the Arab/Muslim world generate animosity and fuel the current negative perception of Israel.

The US Library of Congress has more than seven thousand titles relating to the conflict. This book is not adding to that number; it is not intended to be a treatment of the conflict. However, the conflict, terrorism, and Israel's security measures warrant our consideration, especially if we want to compare Israel to other nations and the Arab–Israeli conflict to other modern conflicts. The Arab riots of 1920,[35] followed by the Hebron massacre of 1929,[36] were the beginnings of Arab terrorism (against Jews and Arabs),[37] and it continues until today.[38] The 1948 War of Independence created a Palestinian refugee population, and this population has become a focal point of the Arab–Israeli conflict. Israel had several wars with Arab neighbors following 1948, but these wars were essentially traditional military campaigns with national players. When military victory was no longer a viable option, aggression reverted to the terrorism of the 1920s.

Between 1987 and 1993 Israel experienced what is commonly known as the first *intifada* (uprising), a period of violent demonstration ending with the Oslo Peace Accords. The second intifada, also known as the al-Aqsa intifada, began waves of suicide bombings that left dozens of civilians dead and hundreds maimed and wounded. In response to ongoing terrorism, Israel began the construction of a security barrier that would separate Israel from the West Bank. The barrier, receiving considerable support from the Israeli public and approval from the Israeli Supreme Court, has been as effective as it is controversial.[39]

The conflict is not one-sided. Israel has made many mistakes, and Palestinian grievances are not completely unjustified. However, we must recognize the bigger picture before we examine and evaluate the smaller pieces of the puzzle.

Israel is not alone in employing a physical deterrent to protect innocent civilians—as any sovereign rightfully should. One of many examples is the Line of Control (LoC) separating India from Pakistan. The LoC is essentially the same apparatus as Israel's security fence: it uses an electrical fence, patrol roads, and barbed wire. The one significant difference is the LoC has land mines.

LOC: INDIA/PAKISTAN	SECURITY BARRIER: ISRAEL/JUDEA AND SAMARIA (WEST BANK)
340 miles	430 miles
Barbed wire	Barbed wire
Trenches	Trenches
Patrol road	Patrol road
Electronic sensors	Electronic sensors
Land mines	No land mines
0 percent concrete	10 percent concrete

Moving from Asia to other Middle Eastern examples, we can find separation barriers in Kuwait, Saudi Arabia, and Egypt. Following the Iraqi invasion of Kuwait, the UN constructed a separation barrier between Kuwait and Iraq in 1991. More recently, in 2004, the Saudis began constructing a separation barrier on its Saudi–Yemen border to stop the unauthorized movement of people and goods. Finally, Egypt began constructing the Egypt–Gaza barrier in December 2009. According to Egypt's foreign minister, Ahmed Aboul Gheit, the separation barrier will defend Egypt "against threats to national security."[40] Gaza is entirely inhabited by Palestinians. Where is the international outcry against Egypt's separation barrier? Egypt is justified in protecting itself "against threats to national security," but Israel, when attempting similar means of protection (from the same people group), receives international scorn. A double standard is apparent.

I rarely visit Israel without spending time in the West Bank. I'm familiar with the way the security barrier and checkpoints affect people's livelihood. It's a problem. Understandably, Palestinians don't want it and neither do most Israelis. Unfortunately, the removal of such security measures will result in the deaths of innocent Israelis, and its presence has protected them. Israel security forces, in the eight months from January to August 2015, prevented seventeen suicide attacks and eight kidnappings.[41] Over a cup of Turkish coffee during my last visit to the West Bank, a Palestinian friend was actually expressing his appreciation for Israeli security measures. With the expansion of ISIS, Palestinians in the West Bank find themselves more secure than their fellow Palestinians in the region. My friend's gratitude was isolated and specific, but his point cannot be dismissed: Israeli security protects both Israelis and Palestinians. I go through the checkpoints by car and on foot. I've gone in and out of the main Bethlehem checkpoint dozens of times, and many of the groups I bring to Israel join me to experience it for themselves. Security measures shouldn't be ignored, and justifiable "threats to national security" don't absolve our need to evaluate the situation. The conclusion after dozens of passages through the checkpoint is that I spend more time waiting in line at a TSA security gate than I do at an Israeli checkpoint.

During Ramadan (the Muslim holy month) in June 2015, I was staying with friends in Beit Jala, a suburb of Bethlehem. One evening, I walked through the main checkpoint. The lines were long, as people were making their way to Jerusalem for Ramadan celebrations. It took me six minutes. There were at least a hundred other people passing through at the same time, and I saw women and children move to the front of the line and exit without presenting any documentation or identification. Two days after my six-minute passage through the checkpoint, an Israeli soldier serving at the Bethlehem checkpoint was stabbed by a woman.[42] Israel's security measures have real consequences on both sides, which I don't ignore for a second. But the security fence and checkpoints are not the fundamental issue.

Continuing with our comparisons, we'll examine casualty totals to see how the Arab–Israeli conflict stands up to other regional and/or modern conflicts. The estimated deaths in the Arab–Israeli conflict, from the Arab riots in 1920 to the present, are 106,153, Jewish and Arab casualties combined.[43] North Korea, on the other hand, is responsible for as many as thirty times that number from 1953 to the present. Between 1917 and 1987 the USSR killed more than 61 million people, not including casualties of war. That's 61 million victims of genocide, politicide, and mass murder![44] The discrepancy between Israel and these two murderous entities is nearly incomprehensible.

In 2011 Syria entered into a devastating civil war. The UN reported deaths nearing two hundred thousand in August 2014.[45] The casualties in Syria are 150 times that of the global Ebola death toll, equivalent to all war-related deaths in Iraq from the 2003 invasion to present, and comparable to the 9/11 attacks—if it happened sixty-four times![46] Furthermore, if the same rate of casualties in Syria was applied to the duration of the Arab–Israeli conflict (1920–2015), the death toll would exceed 4.5 million.

The Arab–Israeli conflict is just that: a conflict between its Arab neighbors, and Palestinians in particular. When we talk about the casualties of the Arab–Israeli conflict, this incorporates Jordanians, Syrian, Egyptians, Iraqis, Lebanese, and Palestinians. Israel, however, is not the only Middle Eastern nation with a history of discord with Palestinians. Jordan (similar to Syria, Lebanon, and Egypt) has a history of problematic relations with Palestinian populations in their borders. Black September is perhaps the foremost example of this history. In September 1970 Jordanian forces killed an estimated 15,000 Palestinian combatants and left between 50,000 and 100,000 Palestinians homeless.[47] In one month Palestinian casualties surpassed the total Arab casualties (including Palestinians and five Arab nations) during Israel's War of Independence between May 1948 and November 1949. Furthermore, between 1987 and 2014, there were 2,014 Palestinian casualties caused by other Palestinians;[48] people were "stabbed, hacked with axes, shot, clubbed and burned with acid."[49] Many of these deaths were a result of what is known as "collaborating" with Israel. Collaborators are any parties with real or perceived interaction with Israelis. In one case is an example showing the severity of these accusations and the preposterous disproportion of consequence: "in October of 1989, a Palestinian father of seven was knifed to death in Jericho after selling floral decorations to Jews who were building a succah."[50]

PALESTINIAN REFUGEES

We've touched on casualties and separation barriers; we'll conclude with population transfers, Palestinian refugees, and how they compare to other forcibly displaced people groups. The Palestinian refugee situation remains a priority in peace talks and global opinion, with obvious consequences for the future of the Palestinians.

According to the United Nations High Commissioner for Refugees (UNHCR), there are approximately 52 million forcibly displaced people in the world, and this figure does not include Palestinian refugees. At the time of this writing, 40 percent of Syria's population are refugees, and reports suggest that China has upwards of 100,000 Korean refugees. This is not a Palestinian or Middle Eastern issue; it's a global, human issue. Consider the following refugee and/or forcibly displaced people groups created since World War II (comparisons will be made with groups larger than the estimated 750,000 Palestinian refugees of 1948 and cases involving Palestinian and/or Israeli populations):

- 1944–50: World War II—12 million displaced Germans[51]

- 1947: Partition of India—14 million displaced[52]

- 1947–48: Jewish refugees from Arab and Muslim countries—850,000[53]

- 1975–79: Phnom Penh—Khmer Rouge displaces over 2 million.[54]

- 1983-Present: Sudan – In 2015 the UNHCR reported over 2 million internally displaced persons.[55]

- 1984–1999: Turkey–PPK conflict—The Internal Displacement Monitoring Centre accounts for 954,000 – 1.2 million forcibly displaced persons with NGOs reporting as many as 3 million.[56]

- 1991: Kuwait—200,000 Palestinian refugees denied return after Iraqi occupation, 200,000 expelled.[57] (In 1981, over 20 percent of Kuwait's population was Palestinian. By 1995 Palestinians represented .01 percent of the population.[58] Yasser Arafat stated, "What Kuwait did to the Palestinian people is worse than what has been done by Israel to Palestinians in the occupied territories."[59])

- 1994: Rwanda – 2 million refugees.[60]

- 2005: Disengagement—Israel dismantles Israeli military installations in Gaza and relocates 9,000 Israelis from 25 settlements in Gaza and Samaria (West Bank).[61]

- 2011—present: Syrian Civil War—9 million refugees[62] (the Palestinian Refugee camp Yarmouk outside of Damascus, Syria, had a population of 127,000. As of this writing it is 18,000.)[63]

- 2014—present: ISIS has internally displaced 2.5 million Iraqis.[64]

There is one major distinction reserved for Palestinian refugees: they are the only refugee population to have their own classification, extending refugee status to children and grandchildren. Consequently, a refugee population that began at 750,000 is now over 5.5 million people! No other refugee population in history has continued its refugee status for three consecutive generations. What's more conspicuous is the amount of humanitarian aid these second- and third-generation refugees have received from the international community over the past sixty-seven years. Another unique characteristic of the Palestinian refugee population is that they have their own UN agency just for them: one agency to tend to 52 million worldwide and another to deal with a population of 5 million. The United Nations Relief and Works Agency (UNRWA) is tasked with the Palestinian refugee population. Considering that the UNRWA has an annual budget of more than half a billion dollars, that it began in 1949, and that its mandate has ballooned from 750,000 people to more than 5 million, it would seem that transitioning Palestinians out of refugee status is not their concern.

The Palestinian refugees, with their exclusive classification, have received more than twenty-five times more international aid per capita than all the monies granted to European countries under the Marshall Plan following World War II; with difference of $7,245 per capita.[65] A total of seventeen nations received the equivalent of $126 billion for more than 240 million people under the Marshall Plan while foreign aid to Palestinians accounts for $31 billion for 4 million people.[66]

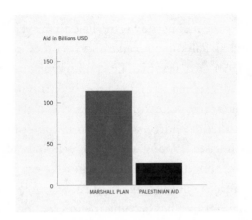

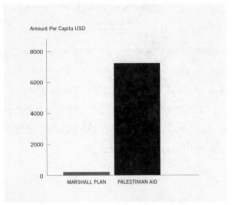

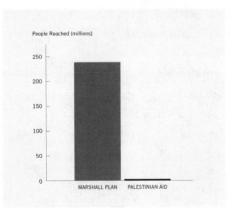

The grotesque incongruity is the Palestinian refugees remain impoverished as Palestinian leadership becomes extraordinarily wealthy. In 1994 the Palestinian Liberation Organization[67] (PLO) had investments valued at approximately $10 billion.[68] Hamas officials in Gaza have gone from rags to riches since Hamas took control, with billions under management and multimillion-dollar real estate purchases.[69] Along with UNRWA, it would seem that improving the conditions of Palestinian refugees and elevating their status are also not the concern of Arab leaders. Nonetheless, the Palestinian refugee has become the international mascot for the oppressed and the disenfranchised, essentially serving as the world's beloved "underdog."[70] This perception of the Palestinians has significant consequences on how the church and the world relate to this issue. And in many ways both have been trained to think and feel a certain way. The Palestinians have received guidance regarding terminology and themes for their movement. In 1967, Muhammad Yazid, a former Algerian minister of information, offered the following advice:

> Wipe out the argument that Israel is a small state whose existence is threatened by the Arab States, or the reduction of the Palestinian problem to a question of refugees; instead, present the Palestinian struggle as a struggle for liberation like the others.
>
> Wipe out the impression . . . that in the struggle between the Palestinians and the Zionists, the Zionist is the underdog. Now it is the Arab who is oppressed and victimized in his existence because he is not only facing the Zionists but also world imperialism.[71]

With billons in international aid and unprecedented world-wide attention and sympathy, the Palestinian refugee still exists, and the blame is placed squarely on Israel, not on Arab nations perpetuating the refugee status of Palestinians. Nor on the Arab nations that encouraged Palestinians to leave their homes during Israel's War of Independence in 1948, making them refugees, only to deny them citizenship after Israel's victory.[72] Not on the UNRWA. Not on the PLO or the Palestinian Authority that administers the West Bank, or Hamas, controlling Gaza. No, Israel is the culprit!

Tragically, "in the West, many politicians, scholars, and activists only use [Palestinians] as a weapon against Israel, as most of the Arab counties have been doing for decades."[73] The cause and the continuation of the Palestinian refugee problem are clear to Arab leaders. The prime minister of Syria in 1948, Khalid al-Azm, listed in his memoirs, published in 1973, what he thought were the reasons for the Arab failure in 1948. Among them was "the call by the Arab governments to the inhabitants of Palestine to evacuate it and leave for the bordering Arab countries . . . We brought destruction upon a million Arab refugees by calling on them and pleading with them to leave their land."[74]

In March 1976, Mahmud Abbas was quoted in *Falastin a-Thaura*, the official journal of the Beirut-based PLO, as saying, "The Arab armies entered Palestine to protect the Palestinians from the Zionist tyranny but, instead, they [Arab armies] abandoned them, forced them to emigrate and to leave their homeland, and threw them into prisons similar to the ghettos in which the Jews used to live."[75]

Despite Israel's meritorious and exemplary accomplishments for a nation not yet one hundred years old,[76] Israel is seen as having negative influence on the world. During the sixty-first session of the United Nations General Assembly (2006–2007), Israel was condemned twenty-two times while Sudan went without a single condemnation for genocide in Darfur.[77] Approximately 40 percent of United Nations Human Rights Council (UNHRC) condemnations are placed on Israel. Out of 191 nations, Israel receives nearly half of the UNHRC condemnations, more than any repressive nation, and in outrageous disproportion to the deaths occurring in the Arab–Israeli conflict.[78] At the time of this writing, the following nations belong to the UNHRC: China, Cuba, Russia, Saudi Arabia, Pakistan, and Venezuela. In shocking contradiction to its conduct as a nation, Israel is the only nation on the planet forced to defend its very right to exist! According to international law, Israel's legal right to reconstitute a Jewish homeland within the boundaries of the Jewish people's ancestral home predates the formation of the United Nations.[79] The natural mind cannot comprehend the world's illogical disposition toward Israel.

If world opinion is increasingly opposed to the land of Israel and the Jewish people, how has the church influenced that view? Perhaps the better question is, how has the church been influenced by the world and forces not of this world?

5

REFLECTIONS OF THE INVISIBLE

I believe in the supernatural. That said, I don't have super-natural experiences on a regular basis. I don't have the book of Revelation figured out, I haven't identified the Antichrist, and I've yet to have an angelic visitation. While I'm still waiting for that angelic encounter, I wholeheartedly believe that angels are real. If I'm going to take the Bible seriously, I have to consider the reality of angels, demons, and an unseen spiritual realm. The presence of these forces should be incorporated into the way I see the world, even if I can't see them.

Angels are present throughout Scripture, and accounts of angelic activity continue to this day. Hebrews 1:14 tells us that angels are "ministering spirits sent out to serve for the sake of those who are to inherit salvation." Chances are you've heard of a missionary protected by angels doubling as guards, or strangers appearing with some type of assistance, never to be seen again. Of all the biblical mentions of angels and demons, one in particular stands out and provides valuable insight into the function of these unseen spiritual agents.

The book of Daniel is full of miracles, dreams, visions, and angelic encounters. For the sake of our discussion, the encounter recorded in Daniel 10 is particularly noteworthy. There we find Daniel at the bank of the Tigris River, being visited by an angelic figure that Daniel describes in a manner remarkably similar to the descriptions given by the prophets Isaiah and Ezekiel.[1] The angel's remarks to Daniel provide us a glimpse into the activity of the spiritual realm:

> Then he said to me, "Fear not, Daniel, for from the first day that you set your heart to understand and humbled yourself before your God, your words have been heard, and I have come because of your words. The *prince of the kingdom of Persia* withstood me twenty-one days, but *Michael, one of the chief princes,* came to help me, for I was left there with the *kings of Persia,* and came to make you understand what is to happen to your people in the latter days. For the vision is for days yet to come." . . . Then he said, "Do you know why I have come to you? But now I will return to fight against the *prince of Persia*; and when I go out, behold, *the prince of Greece* will come. But I will tell you what is inscribed in the book of truth: there is none who contends by my side against these except *Michael, your prince.* (Dan. 10:12–14; 20–21; emphasis added)

Here we find a cast of characters: the angel talking to Daniel, the prince of Persia, Michael, the kings of Persia, and the prince of Greece. Michael and the angel speaking to Daniel are the good guys: the others mentioned are the bad guys, and apparently these demonic forces are associated with (presumably having influence over) geographic areas.[2] Additionally, Michael is referred to as Daniel's prince, suggesting that both the good and the evil agents have assignments. This glimpse into the unseen reveals the spiritual battle between forces of good and evil. We also learn that Daniel's actions in the natural world had consequences in the spiritual world. Namely, his prayers triggered something in the heavens. I wonder what was going on in Daniel's mind when he realized that his prayers were not only heard by God but also causing battles in the heavens!

The power of prayer and the spiritual battle it influences is not a foreign concept to the New Testament. The apostle Paul speaks acutely to this issue in his letter to the Ephesians:

> And you were dead in the trespasses and sins in which you once walked, following the course of this world, following the *prince of the power of the air*, the spirit that is now at work in the sons of disobedience. . . .

For we do not wrestle against flesh and blood, but against the rulers, against the authorities, against the cosmic powers over this present darkness, against the spiritual forces of evil in the heavenly places. (Eph. 2:1–2; 6:12; emphasis added)

Here we find a New Testament reference to a "prince" and a description of what we observed in Daniel 10: spiritual forces in heavenly places. What's important to recognize is that people have the power to influence these spiritual forces, and they can also be subject to their influence. Notice in Ephesians 2:2 that Paul says the Ephesians were "following the prince of the power of the air." The actions of spiritual forces have consequences in the natural world, and the actions of natural forces (people) have consequences in the spiritual world.

It stands to reason that if God has an ultimate intention, the aim of evil spiritual forces would deter individuals and people groups from that intention. Their goal is to keep humanity from what matters most: the knowledge of God.[3] These evil spiritual forces, these cosmic powers, influence the way people think, what they believe and in turn, how they live. Individual thought leads to collective thought, and both yield behavior, lifestyle, and ultimately culture.

INFLUENCE, ABOVE AND BELOW

Prayer isn't the only stimulus that we send into the heavens. Lifestyle, and the daily decisions governed by it, impacts the unseen world as well. Powers in heavenly places lead people away from the knowledge of God through belief systems, "isms," and "ologies"; their resultant lifestyles empower those same spiritual forces. These culture-producing human actions and behaviors often serve to fuel the very power or principality that encouraged the behavior in the first place. As early as the book of Genesis, we can see the collective actions of people having consequence in the heavens. As God is making his covenant with Abraham in Genesis 15, he foretells the Egyptian bondage and return to the Promised Land, saying, "And they [Abraham's descendants through Isaac] shall come back here in the fourth generation, for the iniquity of the Amorites [idolatry] is not yet complete" (Gen. 15:16). Scripture, through both Moses and Paul, considered idolatry (namely sacrifice) participation with demons (Deut. 32:17; 1 Cor. 10:20). I would argue that today idolatry remains and sacrifice (at least in the Western world) has mutated into a more culturally acceptable and often subtle form.

Take climate change, for example. Individuals and nations

are going to great lengths to address this issue. One can argue that the prioritization of the environment is a form of worship. In ancient Israel, when kings worshipped the gods of the nations, altars were made "under every green tree" (2 Chron. 28:4). In addition to worship that venerated nature, the worship of Molech demanded child sacrifice, comparable to modern systems of thought or religion that abuse or end the lives of children (such as sex trafficking), indoctrination of radical Islam, and abortion. Ultimately, *sacrifice* and *worship* are interchangeable, and lifestyle is the currency of both. Lifestyle is a form of worship.[4]

Western scholarship has only recently deviated from the historic understanding of Paul's references to powers and principalities in an effort to demythologize their existence and interpret them as religious, political, or economic structures. What is more consistent with Paul's view is that these "powers exert their influence over the structures" of religion, government, and economy, and those structures "have an ontological point of reference in time, space and history."[5] This trend of demythologization also touches on Paul's use of "air" in Ephesians 2:2. New Testament scholar Clinton E. Arnold, in his very fine book *Powers of Darkness*, speaks to the error of this interpretation:

> The references to "air" and "spirit" are not references to "spiritual climate." When Paul spoke of the "ruler of the kingdom of the air, the spirit who is now at work in those who are disobedient" (Eph. 2:2), a number of interpreters have assumed he was speaking of something like "the climate of opinion." Some would go so far as to suggest that was referring to culture or world view. This does not have long

history in the interpretation of this passage. The origin of this idea can be traced back to an essay written by Heinrich Schlier in 1930 . . . This view has had an undue amount of influence on the course of subsequent treatments on the theme of principalities and powers. The single greatest difficulty with this view is that it would have been unintelligible to a first-century reader . . . Paul is using *spirit* here in the sense of a personal being. Likewise, Paul intended air to be understood in the literal sense; both Jews and Gentiles regarded the air as a dwelling place for evil spirits.[6]

This exchange between the visible and invisible begins in the heavens, and what exists in the heavens (that is to say, forces that are created) can be empowered by what happens on earth. Let's look at earthly examples, normal, everyday scenarios that demonstrate a facet of this dynamic. Whether in small, intimate settings or in massive gatherings of thousands, when people act in a similar manner, it produces something. It could be a support group where the vulnerability and honesty of participants yield an environment of trust and acceptance, a sports event packed with passionate spectators, or a concert with devoted fans.

My neighbor recently attended a Grateful Dead concert at Soldier Field in Chicago, and the place was packed! He struggled to find words to adequately describe the feeling of being with over sixty thousand people singing, dancing, and engaging in other activities associated with a Grateful Dead show. With more than twenty-three hundred performances, the Grateful Dead was known for nonstop touring. Many of their devoted fans, commonly known as Deadheads, would follow the tour for months and even years. Their following became a hippie subculture of sorts. And when they get together for a show, it's a memorable experience, to say the least. Deadheads are a microcosm of how lifestyle and collective behavior create atmosphere. People's actions have power; and, in real time, those actions can generate an atmosphere (a collective emotion or tone) that is felt but yet is still intangible. It's often difficult to articulate and something to be experienced rather than explained. While our senses and the physical elements incorporated into those environments often augment or even create an experience, there are also examples of when the atmosphere is consistent even in the absence of the activity responsible for it. There are places where the cyclical influences of heaven and earth dominate a geographic area.

As I said earlier, I believe in the supernatural. But it's not something I experience on a regular basis, and I've never had an "out of the body" episode (see 2 Cor. 12:3). However, I have had a number of supernatural experiences, and one of them moved me from a place of theoretical to experiential knowledge[7] regarding this topic of spiritual powers, geographic influence, how the actions of people influence the unseen realm, and vice versa.

It was July 2006, and Israel was defending itself against the terrorist group Hezbollah, based in Lebanon and sponsored by Iran. Hezbollah ambushed an Israeli border patrol unit, resulting in the deaths of three soldiers and the abduction of two others. This event escalated into the 2006 Lebanon War, or what can be considered the first round of the Iran–Israel proxy conflict.[8] I was attending an event in Detroit and decided to visit the University of Michigan–Dearborn campus before returning home. The Dearborn campus is home to the Henry Ford estate that sits along the Rouge River and between the Islamic Center of America and the Henry Ford Museum.

The Islamic Center of America is the largest mosque in North America, having a capacity of twenty thousand. Dearborn itself has one of the largest Muslim populations in America. The presence of this community is fueling something in the heavens. Islam is a religious system that is leading people away from the knowledge of God; Muslims are *following* a religious ideology.[9] In Colossians 2:8, Paul warns his readers, "See to it that no one takes you captive by philosophy and empty deceit, according to human tradition, according to the elemental spirits of the world, and not according to Christ." The word for "captive" is the Greek word *sulagōgeō* and refers to war captives being led away as booty. Islam has taken over 1.5 billion people captive through a belief system that is not in "accordance with Christ" (that is, the knowledge of God).[10] To suggest anything else is an error of eternal consequence.

Henry Ford, famous for revolutionizing the car industry, has a very disturbing past marked by his vehement hatred of the Jewish people. In the spring of 1920, Ford made his personal newspaper, the *Dearborn Independent*, to chronicle what he considered the "Jewish menace." Every week, for ninety-one issues, the paper exposed some sort of supposedly Jewish-inspired evil. The most popular and aggressive stories were then chosen to be reprinted into four volumes, called *The International Jew*.[11] Ford also reprinted thousands of copies of the *Protocols of the Elders of Zion*, a book that described an alleged Jewish plan for global control, even though it had by then been exposed as a forgery created in 1903 by the Russian czar's secret police to fan the flames of anti-Semitism.

In an interview with *American Experience*, Hasla Diner

(the Paul and Sylvia Steinberg professor of American Jewish History and professor of Hebrew and Judaic Studies at New York University, and director of the Goldstein-Goren Center for American Jewish History) was asked about Henry Ford's anti-Semitic views and the impact of his public expression of them. Following is an excerpt from that interview:

What kind of things did Henry Ford blame on Jews?

Throughout *The Dearborn Independent*, Ford published articles that would refer to Jews in every possible context as at the root of America and the world's ills. Strikes: It was the Jews. Any kind of financial scandal? The Jews. Agricultural depression? The Jews. So "the Jew," in a way, became the symbol of a world that was being manipulated and controlled.

To me, that's one of the really crucial forces in this rhetoric—that things didn't just happen; but rather somebody is orchestrating these developments, and it's the Jews who are doing it for their benefit. They're doing it in order [to] gain the twin-linked goodies of power and wealth.

Ford also republished the *Protocols of the Elders of Zion*—what is that?

The *Protocols of the Elders of Zion* was a notorious forgery that originally came from Russia, and [was] translated into English. [It] claimed the existence of an international Jewish conspiracy—that a group of Jews got together and basically planned the fate of the world, be it financial catastrophe, be it war. The world was controlled by this little cabal of Jews. [This forgery was] printed in *The Dearborn Independent* as a factual piece. And so someone reading it would take this to be the news.[12]

What's the connection between Ford and the Islamic Center of America? The majority of the Muslim world is decidedly anti-Semitic. According to the Anti-Defamation League's (ADL) global poll on anti-Semitism, the Middle East and North Africa (areas with majority Muslim populations) are decidedly anti-Semitic, with an average of 74 percent of the population harboring anti-Semitic sentiments.[13] Iraq, for example, came in at 92 percent anti-Semitic; 76 percent of those polled maintain that "Jews don't care about what happens to anyone but their own kind," and 75 percent are convinced that "Jews are responsible for most of the world's wars."[14] Earlier I referenced the *Protocols of the Elders of Zion*, printed by Ford's *Dearborn Independent*, the fabrication by Russian czars, first printed in 1903. There are at least nine different Arabic translations available, and it's a best seller throughout the Middle East.[15] I find it hard to believe that coincidence is to blame for the fact that the largest mosque in North America is only a few miles from Henry Ford's estate and the Henry Ford Museum.

Now, we'll return to my visit to the campus. I was in the backyard of the Ford estate, standing on the bank of the Rouge River, and I began to pray for Israel. I was praying from Psalm 83:

> O God, do not keep silence; do not hold your peace or be still, O God! For behold, your enemies make an uproar; those who hate you have raised their heads. They lay crafty plans against your people; they consult together against your treasured ones. They say, "Come, let us wipe them out as a nation; let the name of Israel be remembered no more!" For they conspire with one accord; against you they make

a covenant—the tents of Edom and the Ishmaelites, Moab and the Hagrites, Gebal and Ammon and Amalek, Philistia with the inhabitants of Tyre; Asshur also has joined them; they are the strong arm of the children of Lot. *Selah*

Do to them as you did to Midian, as to Sisera and Jabin at the river Kishon, who were destroyed at En-dor, who became dung for the ground. Make their nobles like Oreb and Zeeb, all their princes like Zebah and Zalmunna, who said, "Let us take possession for ourselves of the pastures of God." O my God, make them like whirling dust, like chaff before the wind. As fire consumes the forest, as the flame sets the mountains ablaze, so may you pursue them with your tempest and terrify them with your hurricane! Fill their faces with shame, that they may seek your name, O LORD. Let them be put to shame and dismayed forever; let them perish in disgrace, that they may know that you alone, whose name is the LORD, are the Most High over all the earth. (Ps. 83:1–18)

I love how this psalm ends. We see what the psalmist, and ultimately God, is really after: the knowledge of God! That's what it's all about, seeking the name of the Lord and acknowledging that He is the Most High over all the earth! We will visit Psalm 83 again in other chapters and glean from its timeless wisdom and prophetic insights.

While Israel was fighting an Iranian-sponsored terrorist organization, I was standing on a riverbank, asking God to "not keep silence," to "not hold your peace or be still," and for Israel and her enemies to seek the name of the Lord. As I began to pray, something happened that has never happened before or since. For the first time in my life, I encountered demonic opposition manifesting in a real-time, tangible manner. As I prayed, my vision began to get blurry and my knees got shaky, so much so that I had to move away from the river's edge for fear of falling in. I continued to pray, and slowly my vision corrected and my strength returned. However, my thoughts were frantic and disoriented. It took extraordinary concentration simply to continue reading the passage of scripture. I had to focus on each word as I spoke it in prayer. It was an experience like none other, and it's difficult to describe.

I had several hours in the car as I made my way back home from Dearborn. As you can imagine, my thoughts were eclipsed by what had just happened. The problem, however, was I didn't know what had just happened! To be quite honest, I was more than a little freaked-out. During that ride home I began to pray, "Lord, what was that?" After the long drive and a lot of prayer and contemplation, I arrived at a conclusion. My conclusion was not solely generated by engaging my natural mind to make sense of the situation; it's something I feel came from the Lord and finds validation in scripture.

What I experienced was an uncontested principality, an evil spiritual force empowered by the lifestyle of the people living in that geographic area who are *following* a cosmic power. In the heavenly places there is war over Dearborn. And in July 2006 it was clear who was winning.

What is seen was not made out of things that are visible (Heb. 11:3). There is a spiritual, invisible origin for what is visible and physical. What we see on earth has its origins in heaven. Intellectual structures and belief systems determine how individuals and people groups behave. These systems are influenced by invisible forces: powers and principalities. There is a strong argument for this in Scripture, and we can identify observable evidence of it. It is not simply unfounded conjecture. This conclusion lends clarity to Scripture. Furthermore, understanding this dynamic is critical to making sense of the illogical position the nations have taken against Israel. It's an explanation for a hatred that surpasses understanding. In the next chapter we will examine further evidence of hatred. However, this hatred will hit much closer to home.

6

A FAMILY FEUD

One of my earliest visits to Israel was for a year of study in
Jerusalem at the Hebrew University's Rothberg International
School. My time there was formative and memorable. Some
memories are fonder to me than others. The one I'm about to
share with you was humiliating. It exposed the naïveté in my
perception of Israel, the Jewish people, and the church. I was
living out of my own story, only familiar with the edges of my
piece of the puzzle and disconnected from the bigger picture.

On the flight from New York to Tel Aviv, I was seated next
to a fellow student who, like most of my peers, was Jewish. As
we talked, I asked her a question. The conversation that followed introduced me to the phenomenon of collective memory.
It also alerted me to the absence of this phenomenon among
Western evangelical Christians. My question was one of genuine
curiosity, not a tactic to divert the topic of conversation to spiritual matters and pigeonhole the girl in a dialogue that would
lead to, "If this plane crashes, will you go to heaven or hell?"

The conversation went something like this:

What do you think about Jesus?

Jesus, I think he's just another historic religious figure . . . like Muhammad.

Well, at least the followers of Jesus love Israel and the Jewish people.

That's when things went bad! I should say that's when I ate some humble pie, and this serving was kosher! To her credit, she was composed and didn't condescend as she let me know that my comment was contrary to about eighteen hundred years of church history! At the time I was a fairly new believer, knew very little of church history, next to nothing of Jewish history, and my church at the time had a very positive view of Israel and the Jewish people. I would go so far as to say that they love Israel and the Jewish people. Prayer for Israel was something that was encouraged regularly, and the land and its people were acknowledged as having great importance to God's redemptive plans. I found their views consistent with Scripture and thought any Bible-believing Christian would come to the same conclusion.

For that young woman it was impossible to separate herself from the long and painful history of Christian anti-Semitism. Like many Jewish people, she saw herself as a part of a people, a people with a history, a people with a memory. The name "Jesus," the image of a cross, or the presence of a church building elicited associations with the Crusades (often referred to as the First Holocaust), inquisitions, pogroms, and the Holocaust itself, all of which happened at the hands of many claiming to be Christians.[1]

If the land and the people of Israel are indelibly linked to God's story, and powers and principalities are at work to keep people from the knowledge of God, one can assume that creating animosity between Gentiles and Jews would be a principal purpose of those powers. How much more so, Gentiles who believe in the God of Abraham, Isaac, and Israel?

The church began as a sect of Judaism. Jesus is Jewish. The apostles are Jewish. Major events after the resurrection of Jesus happen during Jewish holidays and times of prayer in accordance with Second Temple Judaism. In his book *Jewish Roots*, Messianic (a Jewish believer in Jesus) scholar Daniel Juster states:

> After the death of the disciples, leadership among the Jewish believers in Yeshua [Jesus] passed to James' (Jacob's) cousins. By the middle of the second century, however the situation had vastly changed. Great change first occurred between 68 and 100 C.E. Unfortunately, the exact nature of the process is hidden by a lack of sources from this period. However, by the end of this period we see a church and synagogue at war with each other while Messianic Jews were rejected by both groups.
>
> The progress of this split can be mapped in basic terms. First, the New Testament was written in Greek to convey the message of God to a more universal audience. Although the background of the New Covenant was Hebraic, Greeks often applied its content to a Greek context, leading them to adopt teachings and ways of expression that were Greek-oriented. Hence, the Church became more foreign to the Jewish people.
>
> After the death of the Apostles, the leadership of most of the Church passed to non-Jewish leaders. Unfortunately,

many of these leaders did not appreciate Jewish people or the Jewish biblical heritage. The fall of Jerusalem was evidence to them of God's *ultimate rejection* of Israel in spite of Paul's teaching in Romans 11.[2]

Jewish biblical heritage was exchanged for a new approach to Bible interpretation. Instead of a straightforward or literal view of the Scriptures, symbolism and allegory became the norm.[3] This transition to a Greek-oriented mind-set from the Hebraic, in combination with the hostility between the church and the Synagogue, eventually developed into a theology of supersessionism, often referred to as "replacement theology." The basic principle behind this theological view is that the church replaces Israel, and the land and its people are no longer chosen nor are any of the covenantal promises prior to the new covenant in effect. The new covenant replaces the Abrahamic and Mosaic covenants and the Jewish people are just like any other. The *land* and the *people* are stripped of divine promise and purpose.

The paradigms of the Greco-Roman world that displaced a Hebraic view of Scripture assigned intrinsic evil to the natural world, and fueled supersessionism, which created a theological basis for anti-Semitism. The predominantly Gentile church became the Jews' greatest enemy. What began as a family affair turned into a family feud. We can see the arrogance and discord that Paul warned against in Romans 11 as early as the first century. Like tares sown into the harvest, its presence remains in the church to this day:

> For if we are still practicing Judaism, we admit that we have not received God's favor . . . it is wrong to talk about Jesus Christ and live like Jews. For Christianity did not believe

in Judaism, but Judaism in Christianity. —ST. IGNATIUS OF
ANTIOCH (98–117 CE) *EPISTLE TO THE MAGNESIANS*

We too, would observe circumcision of the flesh, your
Sabbath days, and in a word, all your festivals, if we were
not aware of the reason why they were imposed upon you,
namely, because of your sins and the hardness of heart.
The custom of circumcising the flesh, handed down from
Abraham, was given to you as a distinguishing mark, to set
you off from other nations and from us Christians. The
purpose of this was that you and only you might suffer the
afflictions that are now justly yours; that only your land be
desolated, and your cities ruined by fire, that the fruits of
your land be eaten by strangers before your very eyes; that
not one of you be permitted to enter your city of Jerusalem.
Your circumcision of the flesh is the only mark by which you
can be distinguished from other men . . . As I stated before
it was by reason of your sins and the sins of your fathers that,
among other precepts, God imposed upon you the obser-
vance of the Sabbath as a mark. —JUSTIN MARTYR (138–161 CE)
DIALOGUE WITH TRYPHO

We may thus assert in utter confidence that the Jews will
not return to their earlier situation, for they have committed
the most abominable of crimes, in forming this conspiracy
against the Savior of the human race . . . hence the city
where Jesus suffered was necessarily destroyed, the Jewish
nation was driven from its country, and another people was
called by God to the blessed election. —ORIGEN OF ALEXANDRIA
(185–254 CE)

Many, I know, respect the Jews and think that their present way of life is a venerable one. This is why I hasten to uproot and tear out this deadly opinion. I said that the synagogue is no better than a theater and I bring forward a prophet as my witness. Surely the Jews are not more deserving of belief than their prophets. "You had a harlot's brow; you became shameless before all." Where a harlot has set herself up, that place is a brothel. But the synagogue is not only a brothel and a theater; it also is a den of robbers and a lodging for wild beasts. Jeremiah said, "Your house has become for me the den of a hyena." He does not simply say "wild beast" but "of a filthy wild beast" and again, "I have abandoned my house, I have cast off my inheritance." But when God forsakes a people, what hope of salvation is left? When God forsakes a place, that place becomes the dwelling of demons.

—JOHN CHRYSOSTOM (344–407 CE) FROM HOMILY I OF *EIGHT HOMILIES AGAINST THE JEWS*

How hateful to me are the enemies of your Scripture! How I wish that you would slay them [the Jews] with your two-edged sword, so that there should be none to oppose your word! Gladly would I have them die to themselves and live to you! —AUGUSTINE (CIRCA 354–430 CE) *CONFESSIONS*, 12.14

For it is unbecoming beyond measure that on this holiest of festivals [Easter] we should follow the customs of the Jews. Henceforth let us have nothing in common with this odious people . . . We ought not, therefore, to have anything in common with the Jews . . . our worship follows a . . . more convenient course . . . We desire dearest brethren, to separate ourselves from the detestable company of the Jews . . . How, then, could we follow these Jews, who are almost certainly blinded. —THE COUNCIL OF NICEA 325 AD

The previous statement from the Council of Nicea was made to separate Easter celebrations from Passover celebrations. While this transition from "boasting over the root of Israel" to despising it can be documented and traced back to people, places, and philosophies, it still passes understanding. Without the Passover there is no Easter! Passover is central to understanding the initiation of the new covenant: Jesus is waiting to finish the celebration! "I will not drink again of this fruit of the vine until that day when I drink it new with you in my Father's kingdom" (Matt. 26:29).

This view infected the church. Today the symptoms may seem more subtle. In an age of "tolerance," "multiculturalism," and "political correctness," only fringe elements of Christian leadership would make such inciting remarks. Interestingly, the Jews are not the only group believed to exist as witness of God's judgment rather than God's faithfulness. Later on we will see how this idea of a people reserved for earthly punishment touches another member of Abraham's family.

The fruit of this theological error is abundant and damaging. By the grace of God the entire tree has not been spoiled and history has found exceptions. The Puritans of the colonial period (1607–1800) had a deep reverence for Hebraic culture.[4] Puritan theologian John Owen held a belief of the future return of the Jewish people to their homeland.[5] Count Ludwig Zinzendorf, the famous Moravian leader, founded a Messianic Jewish–type community in the 1740s.[6] "The Prince of Preachers," Charles Spurgeon (1834–1892), believed in the physical restoration of

Israel with a national identity, the return of the Jewish people to their ancestral homeland, and Israel remaining spiritually part of the church.[7]

What amazes me is what we find already in scripture that speaks directly to this issue. The clearest example, from the prophet Jeremiah, is immediately following one of the most notable Old Testament promises of the new covenant:

> "Behold, the days are coming, declares the LORD, when I will make a new covenant with the house of Israel and the house of Judah, not like the covenant that I made with their fathers on the day when I took them by the hand to bring them out of the land of Egypt, my covenant that they broke, though I was their husband, declares the LORD. For this is the covenant that I will make with the house of Israel after those days, declares the LORD: I will put my law within them, and I will write it on their hearts. And I will be their God, and they shall be my people. And no longer shall each one teach his neighbor and each his brother, saying, 'Know the LORD,' for they shall all know me, from the least of them to the greatest, declares the LORD. For I will forgive their iniquity, and I will remember their sin no more."
>
> Thus says the LORD, who gives the sun for light by day and the fixed order of the moon and the stars for light by night, who stirs up the sea so that its waves roar—the LORD of hosts is his name:
>
> "If this fixed order departs from before me, declares the LORD, then shall the offspring of Israel cease from being a nation before me forever."
>
> Thus says the LORD: "If the heavens above can be

measured, and the foundations of the earth below can be explored, then I will cast off all the offspring of Israel for all that they have done, declares the LORD." (Jer. 31:31–37, emphasis added)

It's as if God knew a Gentile church would attempt to cast off Israel! In the same breath, He promises the new covenant (made with Judah and Israel) and makes a very clear statement about Israel's future: you can expect the order of the universe to end before you'll see the Jewish people disappear! In case you're wondering, the Hebrew words translated "forever" mean "forever." The literal translation is "all days."

The apostle Paul, in Romans 11:1, also speaks to this issue, "I ask, then, has God rejected his people? By no means!" Not only does Paul emphatically proclaim God's continued purpose; he ups the ante:

So I ask, did they stumble in order that they might fall? By no means! Rather through their trespass salvation has come to the Gentiles, so as to make Israel jealous.

Now if their trespass means riches for the world, and if their failure means riches for the Gentiles, how much more will their full inclusion mean! Now I am speaking to you Gentiles. Inasmuch then as I am an apostle to the Gentiles, I magnify my ministry in order somehow to make my fellow Jews jealous, and thus save some of them. For if their rejection means the reconciliation of the world, what will their acceptance mean but life from the dead? (Rom. 11:11–15)

Israel's "trespass" yielded the salvation of the Gentiles, "their rejection means the reconciliation of the world," and their salvation will result in "life from the dead"! That's kind of a big deal! If that's not having a purpose, I don't know what is. Supercessionism renders Romans 11 unintelligible. Without any distinction between Israel (Jews) and the Gentiles, it simply doesn't make sense. Paul rounds out his focus on Israel with awe and wonder as he considers the mysterious and miraculous ways of God: "Oh, the depth of the riches and wisdom and knowledge of God! How unsearchable are his judgments and how inscrutable his ways!" (Rom. 11:33)

Similar to Jeremiah 31:34 and the importance of reading the next verse, we have another great "next verse" scenario as we transition from Romans 11 to Romans 12. Ignore the "interruption" and read it together:

> For the gifts and the calling of God are irrevocable. For just as you were at one time disobedient to God but now have received mercy because of their disobedience, so they too have now been disobedient in order that by the mercy shown to you they also may now receive mercy. For God has consigned all to disobedience, that he may have mercy on all. Oh, the depth of the riches and wisdom and knowledge of God! How unsearchable are his judgments and how inscrutable his ways!
>
> "For who has known the mind of the Lord, or who has been his counselor?" "Or who has given a gift to him that he might be repaid?" For from him and through him and to him are all things. To him be glory forever. Amen.
>
> I appeal to you therefore, brothers, by the mercies of God, to present your bodies as a living sacrifice, holy and acceptable to God, which is your spiritual worship. Do not be conformed to his world, but be transformed by the

renewal of your mind, that by testing you may discern what is the will of God, what is good and acceptable and perfect.

For by the grace given to me I say to everyone among you not to think of himself more highly than he ought to think, but to think with sober judgment, each according to the measure of faith that God has assigned. For as in one body we have many members, and the members do not all have the same function, so we, though many, are one body in Christ, and individually members one of another. (Rom. 11:29–12:5)

Did you recognize Romans 12:1, the bumper sticker/refrigerator verse? Have you ever considered what Paul meant by "therefore"? Let me suggest a reasonable interpretation: Paul is appealing to the Gentile church to present themselves as living sacrifices because of everything he just said about Israel in chapters 9–11. In this book's previous chapter, we saw how the world views Israel and the Jewish people. Could it be that when Paul makes this statement, it's not simply a vague generalization about being "conformed to the world," but he is actually talking specifically about Israel?

Furthermore, if powers and principalities are at work to keep the Gentile church and Israel from fulfilling their purpose, which will result in "life from the dead," we should anticipate that when the *land* and the *people* start to come back together (as we observed in chapter 3), cosmic evil forces would literally unleash hell.

Animosity toward the Jewish people was sadly, but unmistakably, shaped by Christian theology; however, it also predates Jesus and the existence of the church. The book of Esther is just one of the biblical accounts of ancient endeavors to eradicate the Jewish people.[8] After shameful and horrific centuries of Christian anti-Semitism, hatred of the Jews eventually "mutated" from superstition to science, from religion to race. In this mutation, racial "anti-Semitism" was born.

Ironically, logic, culture, and the sophistication of "Enlightened" Europe set the stage for anti-Semitism to crescendo to the hell that was Hitler, Nazism, and the Holocaust. That crescendo happened in tandem with Jewish immigration to Israel and the First and Second World Wars. This wasn't an evil cosmic assault on just one race; it was an attack on the human race. As stated earlier, the devil is not creative; he's a counterfeit. God separated one people and one place in order to unite all people and all nations. Hence, the unseen forces in heavenly places sought to destroy both while maintaining a clear focus on the original people of covenant: the Jews. Approximately 3 percent of the world's population was killed in World War II, and approximately 40 percent of the world's Jewish population was murdered during the Holocaust.

Waves of Jewish immigration took place between 1882 and 1923. Hitler's *Mein Kampf* was published in 1925; he took power in 1933; and by 1935 the Nuremberg Laws were passed. The Nazi's first state-sanctioned mass murder of Jews took place in 1938. By 1939, the systematic extermination of the Jewish people was under way: the result was the eventual death of 6 million Jews. In Hebrew, the Holocaust is called *ha Shoah*, meaning, "the catastrophe."

Anti-Semitism has taken another turn, and large portions of the church are being swept out in the tide. Before 1948 (and the reestablishment of a Jewish homeland within the ancestral boundaries of Israel), the only element of God's promise to Abraham available to the malicious focus of powers and principalities was the *people*. With the presence of a Jewish state, the focus could include both the *people* and the *land*—enter "anti-Zionism." What was unacceptable through religious paradigms due to the Enlightenment morphed into a racial paradigm.[9] Now that a racial paradigm is no longer palatable in a cultural climate of "tolerance" and "multiculturalism," the latest face of anti-Semitism is political. No longer is it in vogue to hate Jews and justify their ethnic eradication, but it's all the rage to call for the end of the Jewish state, a *political* entity. From Brussels to Riyadh, from the UC Berkeley quad to the World Council of Churches,[10] anti-Zionism is the norm.

CHRISTIAN CRITICS AND UNBIBLICAL CRITICISM

While living in Israel, I began to investigate the Arab–Israeli conflict, and I had the privilege of befriending Palestinians and Israeli Arabs. Those relationships helped me identify my bias toward Israel and the Jewish people. By God's grace I began to move toward a fuller understanding of God's heart for the Arab world, and, specifically, for the Palestinians. Since then, the welfare and future of the Palestinian people remain on the forefront of my heart. I try to look at the Arab–Israeli conflict from multiple angles and perspectives. I have given compassionate consideration to Israel's critics, especially those who share my love for Jesus. While the amount of content in print and online regarding the Arab–Israeli conflict is vast, I find the consistent representation of Christian criticism upholds two elements that deserve our attention.

First, the presentation of information begins with the

individual and attempts to explain the story from a personal perspective. This is not a matter of literary style but, rather, the empowering of personal perspective and personal experience to a fault. Instead of the larger, big picture (metanarrative) informing their story, their story informs the big picture. Experience often serves as a signpost, but it should never be a compass!

Second, I find a consistent implication or outright accusation of conspiracy and scandal coupled with an unrealistic criticism of the events and the parties involved. Utopian ideals about human nature and geopolitical norms generate an undue burden of judgment. This view gives an overinflated sense of self-righteousness to the critics, who are often spectators, and this burden is reserved only for Israel. Arab parties are spared. Furthermore, this criticism is given a theological validity, which is unwarranted and simply disagrees with the biblical narrative and the progression of redemptive history.

One Christian thought leader has authored several books dealing with Israel and serves as the New Testament chair for one of America's leading evangelical colleges. In the first chapter of his book *Whose Land? Whose Promise?* Gary Burge (just before describing his experience as an exchange student in Beirut, Lebanon, in 1973 during the Lebanese civil war) says:

> Certain memories remain fixed in the imagination. They are personal and they become indelible symbols as they help us to understand what transpired in our past. Each of us lives with an archive of such memories, and occasionally we redraw those landscapes, we reconstruct those conversations and crises, making them seem as though they happened yesterday. In some fashion, their power is still with us.[11]

Later on in the same chapter, Burge speaks of his Palestinian roommate and how they "*spent the days and nights talking about what these things meant.*" There was Burge, a young college student watching "jets strafing the refugee camps," with a Palestinian narrator sharing his dorm room. It's no surprise that Burge is one of the most outspoken Christian critics of Israel. From his writings it's clear that his experience has a significant influence on how he understands his theology instead of his theology having significant influence on how understands his experience.

Burge is not alone. Among the Palestinian Christian voices, Naim Ateek has gone so far as to develop a "Palestinian theology of liberation" where Scripture's authority is subject to the perspective of the Palestinian Christian!

> For Palestinian Christians, the core question that takes priority over all others is whether what is being read in the Bible is the Word of *God*. For Palestinian Christians, the core question that takes priority over all others is whether what is being read in the Bible is the Word of *God* to them and whether it reflects the nature, will, and purpose of *God* for them. . . . Do the words reflect an authentic and valid message from God to us today? What is eternally true in the Bible and what is conditioned? What is lasting and what is temporal? These are important questions for Palestinian Christians, whose answers will ultimately determine what God is or is not saying to them in the Bible.
>
> Palestinian Christians are looking for a hermeneutic that will help them to identify the authentic Word of *God* in the Bible and to discern the true meaning of those biblical texts that Jewish Zionists and Christian fundamentalists cite to substantiate their subjective claims and prejudices.[12]

Where Burge's theology is influenced by experience, Ateek's experience is the platform to construct a theology. Ateek decidedly elevates experience over Scripture. When theological reasoning of this sort is at work, inevitably an all-encompassing worldview is formed. This brings us to the second characteristic of Christian criticism of Israel: using unrealistic, utopian ideals to judge Israel's behavior and discern modern Israel's prophetic significance.

Ateek's portrayal of the historic/political background of the Arab–Israeli conflict is infused with rhetoric and accusations of betrayal and *Zionist* scheming.[13] He provides a one-dimensional narrative, elements of which are suspect of fabrication but his most grievous error is found in the manner in which his narrative is presented. When Ateek deals with history, he is speaking as a Christian with the objective of presenting a theology. This approach is not only disingenuous; it's dangerous!

In essence, it echoes the response of the religious leaders during Jesus' earthly ministry. Jesus was not the messiah they were looking for because they allowed their personal perspective to inform the metanarrative instead of allowing the metanarrative to inform their personal perspective. Our experience cannot inform our theology. Theology must inform our experience. Ateek's own words clearly demonstrate his position: "I write mostly out of my own personal experience, trying, above all, to reflect on the conflict both biblically and theologically."[14]

The problem is not that Ateek identifies scandal or conspiracy mingled with the return of the Jewish people to their ancestral homeland. My deep concern is that he uses the presence of scandals and conspiracy as a means to invalidate the significance and prophetic quality of that return. Ateek has an up-close and magnified view of the situation. He and his family have also felt the effects of war and have justifiable grievances against Israel. However, we must consider that this most recent return of the Jewish people was just as real, just as human, and just as scandalous as the return brought about by King Cyrus II. The presence of human error and failure doesn't remove modern Israel from the biblical narrative; it doesn't reject their piece of the puzzle; it makes room for it. In this case, however, in the wireless information age, the return is not just up close and magnified for Ateek; it's magnified for all of us.

Additionally, Burge, drawing from Isaiah's Song of the Vineyard (Isa. 5:3–4), calls Israel's "unrighteousness" and "covenant betrayal" grounds for their complete land loss.[15] This charge is narrow and absent of the appropriate consideration of the Abrahamic covenant's eternal and unconditional qualities. To put this in New Testament terms, his accusation is comparable to telling a Christian he will not inherit eternal life because he failed to be "perfect," as Jesus instructs in Matthew 5:48, or for not literally tearing out a lustful eye or cutting off a hand if it "causes you to sin" (Matt. 5:29–30). This self-serving argument abandons the faithfulness of God and the full counsel of Scripture. It denies the character of God found in a covenant of grace, a promise to which God has bound Himself (Heb. 6:13).

Ateek, in his own way, presents a grievous contradiction when he attacks the theological motivations of Zionism and the prophetic merit of the modern state of Israel. He points to the theological position of the 1885 "Pittsburgh Platform," a set of principles drafted by the rabbis of the Reform movement and designed to set that movement apart from Orthodox and Conservative Judaism. The statement receiving his focus deals with "Israel's great Messianic hope" and on this point,

Ateek agrees with the Reform Jewish thought expressed in the Pittsburgh Platform. Ateek, a Palestinian Christian who "trying, above all, to reflect on the conflict biblically and theologically," agrees with Reform Judaism regarding "Messianic hope." The Reform Jewish view of Messiah is one of a Messianic age because Reform Judaism has no concept of a personal Messiah.[16] One of the Reform movement's distinctions is the departure from traditional Jewish views of Messiah, the Messianic Age, and the resurrection. Of all the things that Jews and Christians disagree on, the hope of a physical resurrection is one of the strongest points of agreement! Nonetheless, to strengthen his "biblical and theological" reflections on Israel, he agrees with Reform Jewish theology concerning Israel, hence providing additional evidence of a bias and selective approach to understanding Israel. He begins with the particular, with his piece of the puzzle, instead of the universal, the big picture. This selective agreement serves his purposes of vilifying Zionism and the early Zionist; however, for Ateek to agree with the Reform Jewish understanding of Messiah is to abandon basic Christian theology. He's sacrificing foundational Christian truths on the altar of political agenda and personal perspective.

Like the Jews of Nazareth on the fateful day when Jesus stood up and read from Isaiah, we are up close and personal with events that demand our serious and thoughtful attention. The very existence of the Jewish people and a reestablished Israel are nothing short of miraculous. Acclaimed Bible scholar Walter C. Kaiser Jr. gives us sobering instruction in his contribution to *The Jew First*:

GOD, ISRAEL, AND YOU

It would be wise for the church to once again take another look at how she is carrying out the work of the kingdom and how she is regarding the nation of Israel. Otherwise we will have small victories here and there, but we will miss the full favor of our Lord, who calls us to a much higher biblical standard of performance for the sake of his excellent name and his Jewish people.[17]

We have choices to make and questions to answer. The consequences are quite literally of biblical proportions. Will we settle for "small victories" or run hard after "full favor"? What story will we prioritize? Will we start with the big picture, or our intimate, familiar piece of the puzzle? Whose story are we in, and who are we following?

7

"WHAT IS IT TO YOU? FOLLOW ME!"

After the returned exiles build and dedicate the second temple, Ezra, a scribe, returns to Israel from Babylon. Scripture says he "began to go up from Babylon," and others "went up also to Jerusalem."[1] As we saw in an earlier chapter, when Jewish people immigrate to Israel—when they return—it's called *aliyah*, meaning "to go up." Traveling to Israel, especially to Jerusalem, is an ascent, an uphill journey, literally and figuratively.

In Psalm 125, the topography that the psalmist described is still seen today. When he said, "as the mountains surround Jerusalem," he was being literal. There are real mountains surrounding the city; therefore, no matter what direction from which you come, you have to go *up* to Jerusalem. Hence, Psalms 120–135 are known as Songs of Ascents. Jewish tradition says that the fifteen psalms refer to the fifteen temple steps the Levites would stand on while reciting them. It also speaks of a desire for spiritual ascent, that God would "give us the ability to lift ourselves up to the greatest of heights."[2]

Visiting Jerusalem never gets old, and entering the city always has mystical wonder and paradoxical awe to it as you encounter the ancient, the modern, and the whispers of a promised future. Even the bumper-to-bumper traffic on Israel's route 1 from Tel Aviv to Jerusalem can't diffuse an element of admiration when I come into the city. One of the Psalms of Ascent has given me more of a problem than Jerusalem traffic . . . yes, you read that correctly. Psalm 131 created a real problem for me. Something just didn't add up, and it set me on an uphill journey:

> A Song of Ascents. Of David. O Lord, my heart is not lifted up; my eyes are not raised too high; I do not occupy myself with things too great and too marvelous for me.
>
> But I have calmed and quieted my soul, like a weaned child with its mother; like a weaned child is my soul within me.
>
> O Israel, hope in the Lord from this time forth and forevermore. (Ps. 131:1–3)

The statement "I do not occupy myself with things too great and too marvelous for me" seems to contradict the events of King David's (the psalmist), life. At the time of writing this psalm, he was not yet king and was still in Saul's service. Nonetheless, if David's story had ended with defeating Goliath, he would still find himself among one of the most well-known figures of the Bible. He was a shepherd boy, the youngest of his brothers, who began an illustrious military career as a giant slayer, only then to become a legendary king and known as a man after God's own heart! Contemporary best sellers are still writing about David and Goliath, and the story is indelibly etched into Western civilization.

David's story is one of the great Cinderella stories of the Bible, if not all of history. And we find him here on his meteoric rise to the throne, a throne that God would promise to establish forever. As if that were not "great" or "marvelous" enough, in the tradition of these psalms he is on his way to Jerusalem to worship the God who has made his story possible. How in the world can David, of all people and at this moment of ascending to Jerusalem, say, "I do not occupy myself with things too great and too marvelous for me"? Can you see my struggle with this text? I'm a white guy from New Jersey. I'm not Jewish. I was never anointed as a king and I never killed a giant. But I get excited every time I enter Jerusalem. Jerusalem fits into the category of great and marvelous, and so does David's life. So what's the deal?

My frustration with the earlier verses was compounded when I began looking at commentaries on this psalm: namely, Charles Spurgeon's *Treasury of David*, John Calvin's *Heart Aflame*, and the *Expositors Bible Commentary*. The commentaries were consistent in addressing the importance of humility; that is, not having a proud heart or haughty eyes. They were also consistent in how they dealt with the second half of verse 1, "I do not occupy myself with things too great and too marvelous for me." What was represented nearly everywhere I looked was the issue of presumption and selfish ambition. Again, as with the subject of humility, I agree. However, these insights, while accurate, did not remedy my conflict.

Before I continue, I must make one thing clear: I'm not taking on the likes of Calvin and Spurgeon! I agree with what they contribute to this text, but there was still something missing. Selfish ambition isn't pleasing to God and will inevitably bear rotten fruit, which will poison your future, but what about godly ambition? What about a heart overflowing with a desire to impact the world for the glory of God, faith for the impossible, vision for things never before accomplished, and a resolve empowered by Jesus' victory over the grave? More important, what about Jesus? Isn't He too great and too marvelous for me? Isn't that what makes grace so great, so marvelous, so amazing?

In addition to my perceived discrepancy, I had a growing list of verses from the Gospels and Epistles that further amplified my perplexity:

> From the days of John the Baptist until now the kingdom of heaven has suffered violence, and the violent take it by force. (Matt. 11:12)

> "Truly, truly, I say to you, whoever believes in me will also do the works that I do; and greater works than these will he do, because I am going to the Father." (John 14:12)

> Indeed, I count everything as loss because of the surpassing worth of knowing Christ Jesus my Lord. For his sake I have suffered the loss of all things and count them as rubbish, in order that I may gain Christ and be found in him . . . But one thing I do: forgetting what lies behind and straining forward to what lies ahead, I press on toward the goal for the prize of the upward call of God in Christ Jesus. (Phil. 3:8–9, 13–14)

> And what more shall I say? For time would fail me to tell of Gideon, Barak, Samson, Jephthah, of David and Samuel and the prophets—who through faith conquered kingdoms, enforced justice, obtained promises, stopped the mouths of lions, quenched the power of fire, escaped the edge of the sword, were made strong out of weakness, became mighty in war, put foreign armies to flight. Women received back

their dead by resurrection. Some were tortured, refusing to accept release, so that they might rise again to a better life. Others suffered mocking and flogging, and even chains and imprisonment. They were stoned, they were sawn in two, they were killed with the sword. They went about in skins of sheep and goats, destitute, afflicted, mistreated—of whom the world was not worthy—wandering about in deserts and mountains, and in dens and caves of the earth.

And all these, though commended through their faith, did not receive what was promised, since God had provided something better for us, that apart from us they should not be made perfect. (Heb. 11:32–40)

God has something "better" for us than he had for Abraham, Moses, Daniel, and the heroes of faith, and "apart from us they should not be made perfect"! Are you thinking what I'm thinking? Hebrews 11 classifies as "great matters or things too wonderful for me."

Still perplexed, I turned to the ultimate commentary on Scripture: Scripture itself. I often find that these *problems* in Scripture are actually invitations to begin exploring the text. It's a treasure hunt masterfully designed by the Master Himself; to put it another way, it's an uphill journey, ascension. In this case, I found the solution to my problem was skillfully placed just around the corner in the next few verses:

"But I have calmed and quieted my soul, like a weaned child with its mother; like a weaned child is my soul within me" (Pslam 131:2).

This analogy of a weaned child is our hidden treasure, our jewel of illumination into the shadows of this apparent contradiction. We will examine two aspects of this analogy: first, the proactive, conscious arrival to a *calm* and *quieted* soul or, in other words, contentment; second, we'll examine the position of a child's being *weaned with its mother.*

A CALM AND QUIETED SOUL

Contentment is not a default state of being. This is not an accidental achievement; it's a destination that requires deliberate action. David was a man with a nature like ours. While the passing millennia have created different external circumstances, it has not altered our internal disposition. Modern humanity, at its core, is no different from the bygone days of David and the heroes listed in Hebrews 11. It's a *choice* to be content. And that choice necessitates behavior that agrees with, and testifies to, the decision. Eventually that combination, like sun and water to a plant, will yield the foliage and blossoms of emotion allied with contentment. Your heart will follow your mind and your actions.[3]

LIKE A WEANED CHILD

Recognizing God as our heavenly Father is a topic woven throughout Scripture and uniquely evident in the life and ministry of Jesus. When Jesus taught the disciples to pray, He began, "Our Father." Identifying God as Father, and the corresponding recognition that we are His children, is an essential key to a genuine, life-giving relationship with God.

Countless volumes have been penned and published on this topic, and for us, in dealing with Psalm 131, it's a secondary point. Nevertheless, it's such an integral part of the knowledge of God that it warrants attention. The two aspects of a childlike disposition to which I'll direct our focus are trust and the shameless recognition of need.

A weaned child with its mother provides a beautiful picture of contentment using a universally evocative relationship. This child isn't cuing mom for a meal; he's weaned, and his motivation is not found in his needs. Rather, we see a child contented with his mother. Regardless of the quality of your relationship with your mother, no matter who you are, you have one, and you didn't get to choose her! It's a sovereign choice, decided without your consent or consultation, and it's irrevocable. Therein is the fix to the problem, the last step before the summit of the hill. Contentment with God's sovereignty, being at peace with the choices God makes for you.

What was too great and too marvelous for David? Anything outside God's will for *his* life. Consider again Jesus' teaching the disciples how to pray: "Our Father in heaven, hallowed be your name. Your kingdom come, your will be done, on earth as it is in heaven" (Matt. 6:9–10). God is not keeping us from the great and the marvelous; quite the opposite. He has invited us to it and gone to unimaginable lengths to make it possible for us. In fact, Ephesians 2:10 tells us that He's already done it: "For we are his workmanship, created in Christ Jesus for good works, which God prepared beforehand, that we should walk in them."

Will you, like David, calm and quiet your soul? Will you embrace God's sovereign choices for your life and walk in the good works that have already been prepared beforehand? Like Paul, will you lay hold of God's purpose in His laying hold of you? When you discover that purpose, those good works, will you calm and quiet your soul, like a weaned child with its mother; or, like the prophet Jonah, find yourself going from shipwreck to shipwreck until you embrace the irrevocable calling on your life?

I realize that I have just brought an elephant into the room. Our point of focus is not the mysterious and paradoxical reality of free will and predestination. It's something far more accessible and practical: an obstacle to arriving at this place of contentment with our God-given purpose. That obstacle is distinguishing between *value* and *purpose*. Like having a GPS with dated maps and poor satellite connection, as we navigate the journey of discovering God's will and purpose for our lives, it causes confusion and throws us off course. The confusion between value and purpose can leave us adrift at sea, tossed by the waves of life, and aimlessly seeking God's will. Discerning the difference between value and purpose will update the GPS, strengthen its connection, and make it a trustworthy guide. Finding and embracing God's true north for our lives will deliver us to shores of contentment. It also has a great deal to do with Israel.

VALUE AND PURPOSE

In the grand scheme of things, David wasn't all that different from you and me, and neither were the disciples. If you look for it, you'll discover the personalities of these men as you read the Scriptures. They were real, everyday people who happened to change the world.

Peter has a personality that's hard to miss. Scripture describes his epic victories and heartbreaking failures. With rarely anything middle-of-the-road, Peter seems to always find himself at one of two extremes. Peter's worst moment comes during the events leading to Jesus' crucifixion. Moments after Jesus is accused of blasphemy by the high priest and the crowd starts calling for His death, Matthew 26 gives the following account:

Now Peter was sitting outside in the courtyard. And a servant girl came up to him and said, "You also were with Jesus the Galilean." But he denied it before them all, saying, "I do not know what you mean." And when he went out to the entrance, another servant girl saw him, and she said to the bystanders, "This man was with Jesus of Nazareth." And again he denied it with an oath: "I do not know the man." After a little while the bystanders came up and said to Peter, "Certainly you too are one of them, for your accent betrays you." Then he began to invoke a curse on himself and to swear, "I do not know the man." And immediately the rooster crowed. And Peter remembered the saying of Jesus, "Before the rooster crows, you will deny me three times." And he went out and wept bitterly. (Matt. 26:69–75)

The guy who got out of the boat and walked on water with Jesus (Matt. 14:29), the one who responded, "You are the Messiah" to Jesus' question, "Who do you say that I am?" (see Matt. 16:16), is now denying he has anything to do with Jesus, to the point of invoking a curse on himself! Thankfully, just like Peter's personality, this story finds another extreme. John 21 provides the account of Peter's restoration and beautifully displays the compassion and mercy available in Jesus. However, it's not long before Peter finds his foot in his mouth again.

Following the resurrection and the disciples' initial encounter with the resurrected Messiah, Peter and the others return home. Peter, being a fisherman, goes fishing. From inside his boat, as the sun began to rise over the hills, he could see the villages where Jesus taught, healed, and delivered. He could see the shoreline where Jesus issued his invitation, "Follow me."

Being familiar with the Sea of Galilee, he could discern where Jesus had calmed the storm and where He had walked on the water—and how he, for a moment, had walked on the water with Him. Peter had walked on the water, and he'd also sunk. After the devastation of denying Jesus three times (just as Jesus had foretold), one can imagine that his thoughts went to the sinking part of that memory and not the walking. Jesus had rescued Peter from the water, and Peter was about to find out that Jesus would also rescue him from his despair:

> Just as day was breaking, Jesus stood on the shore; yet the disciples did not know that it was Jesus. Jesus said to them, "Children, do you have any fish?" They answered him, "No." He said to them, "Cast the net on the right side of the boat, and you will find some." So they cast it, and now they were not able to haul it in, because of the quantity of fish. That disciple whom Jesus loved therefore said to Peter, "It is the Lord!" . . .
>
> When they had finished breakfast, Jesus said to Simon Peter, "Simon, son of John, do you love me more than these?" He said to him, "Yes, Lord; you know that I love you." He said to him, "Feed my lambs." He said to him a second time, "Simon, son of John, do you love me?" He said to him, "Yes, Lord; you know that I love you." He said to him, "Tend my sheep." He said to him the third time, "Simon, son of John, do you love me?" Peter was grieved because he said to him the third time, "Do you love me?" and he said to him, "Lord, you know everything; you know that I love you." Jesus said to him, "Feed my sheep. (John 21:4–7, 15–17)

Three times Peter denied Jesus, and three times he confesses his love. As you might have guessed, this epic win, this transformative moment of redemption and commissioning, is getting ready to swing back to the other extreme. While Jesus and the disciples walk the shore of the Galilee, the pendulum seems to move with each step Peter takes. Soon enough he'll find his foot in his mouth!

The scene of Peter's early morning campfire restoration is followed by Jesus telling Peter (in a way that only Jesus could) how he will ultimately glorify God: in martyrdom. Let's return to the text to see what Jesus tells him and how Peter responds:

> "Truly, truly, I say to you, when you were young, you used to dress yourself and walk wherever you wanted, but when you are old, you will stretch out your hands, and another will dress you and carry you where you do not want to go." (This he said to show by what kind of death he was to glorify God.) And after saying this he said to him, "Follow me." (John 21:18–19)

What's of interest to us is how Peter responds. It's important for us to keep in mind that, like Peter, it's only a matter of time before each of us finds the proverbial foot in our mouth—some of us more often than others, but none of us is exempt from making mistakes. What we find in verses 20 and 21 represent the "Peter" in all of us, a powerful temptation that inevitably comes to everyone:

> Peter turned and saw the disciple whom Jesus loved following them, the one who had been reclining at table close to him and had said, "Lord, who is it that is going to betray you?" When Peter saw him, he said to Jesus, "Lord, what about this man?"

After an intensely personal moment of reconciliation with the resurrected Messiah, which is topped off by the foretelling of the manner of his death, Peter's response to all this is to ask, "What about that guy?" Peter's initial response, and often ours, is comparison. Instead of embracing and reflecting on what the sovereign and merciful hand of the Lord has given to him, he attempts to measure up with the next guy.

Comparison is a temptation that is common to us. But this wasn't about keeping up with the Joneses, your car, your wardrobe, your salary, or your Twitter following. This was about a heavenly calling and eternal purpose! The trap that Peter walks into, or the hand that puts his foot in his mouth, is *comparison* as a means to determine value. This false standard will ultimately deceive us and obscure the contentment found in seeing ourselves in light of who God calls us to be. I love Jesus' response to Peter:

> Jesus said to him, "If it is my will that he remain until I come, what is that to you? You follow me!" So the saying spread abroad among the brothers that this disciple was not to die; yet Jesus did not say to him that he was not to die, but, "If it is my will that he remain until I come, what is that to you?" (vv. 22–23)

Peter and John would have different stories, and each would glorify God with his life and his death. It's all too easy for us duplicate what Peter did in John 21. We can look to our brother or sister in Christ and begin to make comparisons. We can apply the false standard to our own lives and, in turn, we confuse purpose and value. We need to hear Jesus' charge to Peter: "What is that to you? You follow me!" Belonging to Jesus is what gives us value; our purpose is *how* we follow Him. Our purpose is found when we submit our lives to Jesus and He begins to direct our steps and influence the major and minor decisions of our lives. It's a process, an uphill journey of transformation. Following Jesus is something that none of us is worthy of. And, despite our weaknesses, our failures, and our sin, Jesus calls us to follow Him. Nothing is greater or more marvelous than that!

David had a purpose that was great and marvelous, as did Peter, John, and as do you. Our purpose, the *how* of following Jesus, carries the significance and value of the One who created us for that purpose. Your purpose or, again, the *how* of following Jesus, is what Paul spoke of as *laying hold of the reason why Jesus laid hold of him* (see Phil. 3:12). For each of us that will look different. When I recount my journey of purpose, my walking out the *how* of following Jesus, I speak about giving Jesus my "yes." Without knowing what it will look like or having any of the details beforehand, I said yes, and He has been placing me in the right place at the right time every step of the way. The end result is our sanctification, being transformed into the image of Jesus. We follow Him to become like Him, and our heavenly Father knows exactly what path will bring us to contentment. He knows where our piece fits in the puzzle.

Let's return to David and Psalm 131 and look at how I resolved the tension between David's words and his circumstances. David's life was great and marvelous, and I'm convinced that Jesus wants each of us to live a life that is as purposeful as David's. David fulfilled his purpose in his generation (Acts 13:36), and we are called to do the same. None of us, however, can fulfill someone else's purpose or do it in a generation other than the one in which we belong. David's purpose wasn't Saul's purpose, Peter's purpose differed from John's and my purpose (my *how* of following Jesus) will be different from yours. That difference doesn't determine value!

What was too great and too marvelous for David was a purpose that wasn't his. Jesus is calling all of us to something too great and too marvelous: Him. When we embrace the *how*, when we give our "yes" to Jesus, our lives will be greater and more marvelous than we imagined because we're experiencing the life that Jesus planned for us. We're ascending the hill of sanctification and being transformed into the image of Jesus.

Ephesians 2:10, then, tells us that "we are [God's] workmanship, created in Christ Jesus for good works, which God prepared beforehand, that we should walk in them." There are "good works" already prepared for each of us! When we follow Jesus, we accomplish those good works, we fulfill our purpose. When you're tempted to compare yourself to others, remember Jesus' words to Peter: "What is it to you? You follow me."

The great orator and evangelist D. L. Moody said, "There are many of us that are willing to do great things for the Lord, but few of us are willing to do little things." Moody, like David, fulfilled his purpose in his generation, and his statement was spot-on. If your "yes" to Jesus leads you to do seemingly *little* things or great things, *hidden* things or *famed* things, the fact of the matter is that the value of your obedience, the value of your purpose, is the same because we are created in Jesus for good works. Those good works are already prepared for us to walk in.

All of us have a purpose. Story after story in the Bible, hero after hero, and villain after villain suggest that purpose is something that God provides and not something that individuals create. God has something for you to do, and only for you. Our

God-given purpose can't be exchanged; it can only be embraced or neglected. In the same manner, Israel—the *land* and the *people*—serve a purpose that cannot be exchanged, and Gentiles also have a specific purpose. The two are not interchangeable, but each is great and marvelous. The temptation of comparison and the pitfall of confusing value and purpose can pull on the heart and mind of a people just as it can on a person.

SPIRITUAL INHERITANCE

From pastors and average churchgoers alike, I've often heard the statement, "Israel is just another nation like all the rest, and the Jews are just like everyone else. They need Jesus." While I agree that the covenant that Jesus instituted is for both Jew and Gentile, to say that Israel is just like other nations or that the Jews are just like everyone else is an idea that has next to nothing to do with scripture or history. In a previous chapter, we dealt with the unmatched contribution the Jewish people have made to humanity. We also saw how the Jewish people were meant to be a special picture of God's holiness and grace, even to the point of being the conduit through which the Messiah Himself would come to earth in the flesh. The obvious conclusion is that there's no one like them—never has been, and never will be. The difference is due to purpose, a God-given purpose, and that purpose did not expire when the church was born. That purpose, while exclusive to Israel (Jews), does not eclipse the value or purpose of the Gentiles. In fact, by God's design, they work together. We need each other, and the roles of the Gentiles and Israel are not interchangeable.

While it may be cliché, there's a helpful analogy that we'll employ when considering Israel and Gentiles. When presented with this topic of Gentiles and Israel, people often confuse value and purpose, and that confusion is evidenced in questions such as, "Does God love Israel and the Jews more than the church?" My response is not a statement but two questions: "Does a parent with more than one child love or value any of their children more than the other?" The answer is typically "No, there is a love and value enjoyed by all the children." The next question is, "How many firstborn children does that parent have?" The answer: "One." Israel (Jews) is like God's firstborn. He doesn't love the other children less, but there's a difference, and that difference is expressed in *purpose*, not *value*. What often adds to this confusion is the need to distinguish Gentiles, Israel (Jews), and the church. Many times when people refer to the church, what they really mean is Gentiles.

If you don't have children, you still get the point. And if you're not married, you can still appreciate this second analogy. My wife has a spiritual heritage from her family, and she represents four generations of faithful commitment to the Lord. I, on the other hand, represent only a second generation of faith. When I married her, I joined her spiritual heritage, a heritage that did not naturally belong to me. Our children, as they choose to follow the Lord, will represent a fifth generation of faith, not a third. Both my children and I benefit from the spiritual heritage of my wife. As a married couple we have a shared purpose as well as individual purposes or roles. Those roles are important and God given. They're both spiritual and natural. Together, my wife and I share the purpose of rearing our children in a godly way. Individually, spiritually as a man, I should function as the "priest" of our home and provide the primary spiritual leadership. Naturally, as a man, I will never assume the role of bearing children. The spiritual and natural roles are in place as designed by God, and following those roles produces the best quality of life as well as positioning us to fulfill our purposes, general and specific.

It's important to understand that my wife and I have both overlapping roles and specific roles. Likewise, Gentiles and Israel (Jews) have both overlapping and specific purposes. There are specific, irrevocable roles that are essential to fulfilling the overlapping purpose.[4] As foolish at it might sound, I could get offended that God chose women to bear children and not men. I could convince myself that God loves women more because they have this experience of bringing life into the world. On the other hand, I could think that He loves men more because they don't have to go through labor . . . I trust you get the point.

Jews and Gentiles are similar. Gentiles benefit from the spiritual heritage of Israel. And yet, my faith, as a Gentile, can complete the faith of the Jewish heroes and saints (see Heb. 11) because I have been joined to a spiritual heritage not naturally belonging to me. After the apostle Paul told the church of Ephesus that they were God's craftsmanship, created in Christ Jesus, he told them to *remember* that they were "alienated at one time from the commonwealth of Israel and strangers to the covenants of promise," ultimately telling us that the church did not replace Israel but has been joined to Israel. Just as my wife and I were joined together in marriage with overlapping and distinct roles, Gentiles and Jews, through the new covenant, have one ultimate purpose but different and nontransferable roles.

The depth and specification of those roles is a topic worthy of its own book. And even the apostle Paul refers to the dynamics of the Gentiles and Israel as a "mystery" (Rom.

11:25) and as demonstrating "the depth of the riches and wisdom and knowledge of God!" (Rom. 11:33). What's clear is that the salvation of the Gentiles and Israel are intertwined, and the two are joined together while maintaining distinct roles. Our purpose is primarily to acknowledge that Israel has an "irrevocable" (Rom. 11:29) calling, distinct from the Gentile church, and the roles of Israel and the Gentiles are both vital to the church's destiny. When those roles are understood and embraced,[5] each can fulfill their purpose, both general and specific. Both children, the firstborn (Jews) and the second born (Gentiles), will find themselves calm and quieted.

Gentiles and Jews have purpose. They have a *shared* purpose when joined together in Jesus as parts of His bride (the church) that does not negate their specific roles. Additionally, Israel (both the land and the people) has a purpose that exists outside of the new covenant. Israel's recognition of Jesus does not negate the eternal and unconditional covenant of grace God made with Abraham, however; only the new covenant is necessary for their ultimate purpose and salvation to be fulfilled. This idea, similar to the value of the Old Testament, also finds representation outside of Protestant views. The Catholic catechism speaks of the "mystery"[6] of the church and her link to the Jewish people,[7] God's "sheer gratuitous love" toward Israel, and the necessity of Israel in God's redemptive plan.[8]

The importance of recognizing this cannot be overstated. Romans 9:6–29 speaks to this issue and should receive your attention as you "think over" these things so that "the Lord will give you understanding" (see 2 Tim. 2:7). Our discussion, however, will return to Ephesians. Paul begins with some of the most breathtaking statements in Scripture as he describes to this

Gentile group of believers their position in Christ:

> Blessed be the God and Father of our Lord Jesus Christ, who
> has blessed us in Christ with every spiritual blessing in the
> heavenly places, even as he chose us in him before the foun-
> dation of the world, that we should be holy and blameless
> before him. In love he predestined us for adoption as sons
> through Jesus Christ, according to the purpose of his will,
> to the praise of his glorious grace, with which he has blessed
> us in the Beloved. In him we have *redemption* through his
> blood, the *forgiveness of our trespasses*, according to the riches
> of his grace, which he lavished upon us, in all wisdom and
> insight making known to us the mystery of his will, according
> to his purpose, which he set forth in Christ as a plan for the
> fullness of time, to unite all things in him, things in heaven
> and things on earth. In him we have *obtained an inheritance*,
> having been predestined according to the purpose of him
> who works all things according to the counsel of his will.
> (Eph. 1:3–11, emphasis added)

Paul goes on to articulate their condition outside of Christ.
Here we find again impressive and frequently quoted portions
of scripture:

> And you were dead in the trespasses and sins in which you
> once walked, following the course of this world, following
> the prince of the power of the air, the spirit that is now at
> work in the sons of disobedience— among whom we all once
> lived in the passions of our flesh, carrying out the desires
> of the body and the mind, and were by nature children
> of wrath, like the rest of mankind. But God, being rich in

mercy, because of the great love with which he loved us, even when we were dead in our trespasses, made us alive together with Christ—by grace you have been saved—and raised us up with him and seated us with him in the heavenly places in Christ Jesus, so that in the coming ages he might show the immeasurable riches of his grace in kindness toward us in Christ Jesus.

For by grace you have been saved through faith. And this is not your own doing; it is the gift of God, not a result of works, so that no one may boast. For we are his workmanship, created in Christ Jesus for good works, which God prepared beforehand, that we should walk in them. (Eph. 2:1–10)

After all this, Paul drops the word that we saw connecting Romans 11 to Romans 12: "therefore"! He takes these earth-shattering, life-transforming statements and uses them to set up his point. His point was to *remember* God's story, to *remember* covenant!

Therefore, remember that at one time you Gentiles in the flesh, called "the uncircumcision" by what is called the circumcision, which is made in the flesh by hands—remember that you were at that time separated from Christ, alienated from the commonwealth of Israel and strangers to the covenants of promise, having no hope and without God in the world. But now in Christ Jesus you who once were far off have been brought near by the blood of Christ. (Eph. 2:11–13)

God's story is the story of Israel—the land and the people—and, through Jesus, the church became part of that story. We didn't start our own story, and God certainly didn't begin a new story. He just kept telling the same one!

At this point, we need to make an important distinction between a *priority* and a *calling*. From Abraham on, all these heroes of faith found themselves in God's story. And their journey to a calm and quieted soul, their place in the story, directly involves Israel and the Jewish people. For you that may not be the case. We all have different roles and functions in the body of Christ. The needs of the broken world around us can be overwhelming, and there is no shortage of opportunities to glorify God in serving others. Israel, the Jewish people, Palestinians, Arabs, or Muslims may have nothing to do with what God has placed on your heart and woven into your destiny. Israel may have nothing, directly, to do with your calling. However, that doesn't mean the land and the people shouldn't be a priority.

Let's consider an example outside of our current context. We'll pretend that I'm called to be a worship leader. For those who know me, this exercise will demand much of their imagination. Worship represents a calling. It's my part of the body, my place of contentment and fulfillment of purpose. While I'm called to lead worship and to cultivate my craft as a musician, I have a priority as a Christian to be a godly steward of my finances. Generosity and stewardship should be a priority in my life. Now let's reverse the example. Let's say that I'm called to marketplace ministry, and finances have a very clear connection to my calling. How I handle money falls in the category of calling as well as priority. As someone called to marketplace ministry, as a Christian, I should still make worship a priority in my life.

God may not call you to Israel, but He has made it a priority, and it should find representation in your life if you desire to live a life that reflects the priorities of Scripture.

Jesus calls us to love Him more than anyone or anything else (Luke 14:26–27). The call to be a follower of Jesus is a call to willfully surrender and submit everything to His wisdom and care. It's a call to elevate our loyalty to Jesus above family, culture, politics, possessions, and identity. Paul considered all things loss for the sake of Christ (see Phil. 3:7–8). He went from killing believers to preaching the glorious mystery of the gospel of Jesus Christ. Nothing was more important than his place in *the story* and the knowledge of God. Oh, that it would be the same for all of us, regardless of our families, culture, possessions, political aspirations, nationalism, and identity! Forsaking all still means forsaking all, and forever still means forever.

We will do well to remember covenant today, to recognize that God's story is still a story of *land* and *people*. Through Christ we've been included, and that inclusion was never to their exclusion. Like many aspects of marriage and family, it's not lacking a sense of mystery and awe (see Rom. 11: 25–36). God's story is a family affair.

8

WILD BLESSING

On a short walk from Jerusalem's Old City, you'll find one of Jerusalem's "must see" buildings, the Jerusalem International YMCA. The stunning architecture is matched by its rich history. Opened in 1933, it was created with the vision of providing expression for the Jewish, Christian, and Muslim communities in Jerusalem. The architecture follows suit with a combination of Byzantine, Romanesque, Gothic, and neo-Moorish styles, bearing witness to traditions of Judaism, Christianity, and Islam. You'll find Gothic vaulted ceilings, painted arabesques, and a seventeenth-century wooden ceiling from Damascus. The building has forty columns representing the forty years of Israel's wandering and the forty days of Jesus' temptation. The twelve tribes, twelve disciples of Jesus, and twelve followers of Muhammad are represented by the twelve windows of the auditorium and the twelve cypress trees in the garden.[1] Under the vaulted ceilings of the YMCA lobby, I met a man whose life represented the most precious and sobering of Christian traditions: risking one's life for the gospel.

I was tasked to do research on Arab Christians and create a prayer guide that would aid believers in their prayers for the Arab world.[2] Pastor Naim Khoury of the First Baptist Church of Bethlehem was gracious enough to meet with me. That meeting was one of my "signposts." It didn't update my GPS or recalculate my route. It was more like God saying, "You're approaching your next turn." Pastor Khoury is a modern-day hero of faith who takes a courageous stand for the gospel in a place that is increasingly hostile to churches that actively evangelize.[3] Bethlehem, similar to Nazareth, is directly associated with the life of Jesus. Also similar to Nazareth, it has undergone a major demographic shift in the last century. The Christian majority in these two places has become a dwindling minority. If nothing is done to secure the Christian presence in Bethlehem, it could disappear in my lifetime.

The naiveté that resulted in the infamous blunder I made on my flight to Israel also perpetuated partiality in my heart toward Israel and the Jewish people. At that stage of my life as a believer, my exposure to what was happening in Israel and the Middle East was very one-sided. Replacement theology doesn't align with Scripture or history, and I never negated the purpose of Israel and the Jewish people. However, I embellished that purpose and allowed that inflated view to eclipse God's purposes for *every* nation, tribe, and tongue. My constricted outlook was quickly called to account during my year in Jerusalem. Through relationships with Palestinian classmates and eventual work with Arab–Israeli and Palestinian Christians, I saw the purposes of God for another people: the Arabs.

FROM A BLESSING TO A CURSE

There is a prevalent and maledictive misunderstanding concerning support for Israel. In part it is colored by a culture that is increasingly polarized on all fronts, and in part by incendiary commentary made by pugnacious Israel advocates. The sad truth is that far too many people conclude that a positive position toward Israel is synonymous with a negative position toward the Arabs: they equate being pro-Israel with being anti-Arab. Nothing could be further from the truth.[4] And contrary to what many critics of Israel and Palestinian sympathizers believe, Israel is more the solution than the problem.

As has been the custom in this book, we'll begin at the beginning and try to make some sense of this misunderstanding and the negative perception of Arabs who, like the Jews, are also Semitic. In doing that, we will discover another form of Christian anti-Semitism. As we'll soon find out, this family affair is not lacking its family issues!

Abraham's first son Ishmael (Gen. 16:15), born to Hagar, is often mistakenly identified as the patriarch of the Arab people. Conversely, Abraham's son Isaac, born to Sarah (Gen. 17:21 and Rom. 9:7), is accurately identified as the patriarch of the Jewish people. The vast majority of the Arab world cannot trace its lineage to Ishmael. However, the perception exists in large part due to Islam's veneration of Ishmael and Islam's Arabization of indigenous populations during Muslim conquest and colonization. Arabic was the language of Islam's imperialist force, and those conquered by it now comprise what we understand as the Arab world.

Some of my dearest friends call Israel home. One of those friends is David Nekrutman. David directs the Center for

Jewish-Christian Understanding and Cooperation (CJCUC) in Efrat, right next to Bethlehem. The CJCUC is the only Orthodox Jewish organization established for theological conversation between the Orthodox community and the evangelical community. It's not just the only one that exists today; it's the only one to exist *ever*!

David is a modern Orthodox Jew and recognizes his work with Christians as nothing less than a divine calling. He's an extraordinary and courageous pioneer in the field of Jewish–Christian relations. Over the years he's become very familiar with Christian theology and thought. I have listened to David speak to groups on numerous occasions. His perspective adds great depth to the Gospels as he clarifies the historic and religious context of the life and ministry of Jesus. I always learn something when David is teaching.

On one particular visit, David and I decided to have a group study session focused on Ishmael. The lecture and discussion would include how Ishmael is understood in the life of the patriarchs and how that influences the way the modern Orthodox community views the Arab world. David often references a felicitous quote from Hayyim Nachman Bialik when we explore Scripture together: "He who reads the Bible in translation is like a man who kisses his bride through a veil." In the case of Ishmael, most English translations are not only veiled brides, they're also bad kissers!

In Genesis 16 we are introduced to Hagar, the female Egyptian servant of Abraham's wife, Sarah. Sarah is barren and urges Abraham to take Hagar as a wife so she can bear him a child. It doesn't take long for this plan to put Sarah at odds with Hagar and, as David aptly puts it, "begins the Bible's first soap opera." Abraham and Sarah's decisions regarding Hagar, and later Ishmael, trouble their household. The ensuing strife will ripple through generations. Many would argue that we are still feeling its effects today.

Hagar flees from her cruel mistress in Genesis 16, and that is where we'll find the puckered lips of a veiled bride:

> [7] The angel of the LORD found her by a spring of water in the wilderness, the spring on the way to Shur. [8] And he said, "Hagar, servant of Sarai, where have you come from and where are you going?" She said, "I am fleeing from my mistress Sarai." [9] The angel of the LORD said to her, "Return to your mistress and submit to her." [10] The angel of the LORD also said to her, "I will surely multiply your offspring so that they cannot be numbered for multitude." [11] And the angel of the LORD said to her, "Behold, you are pregnant and shall bear a son. You shall call his name Ishmael, because the LORD has listened to your affliction. [12] He shall be a wild donkey of a man, his hand against everyone and everyone's hand against him, and he shall dwell over against all his kinsmen." [13] So she called the name of the LORD who spoke to her, "You are a God of seeing," for she said, "Truly here I have seen him who looks after me." (Gen. 16:7–13)

Verse 12, taken by itself, sounds like a curse if I ever heard one! How would you feel if an angel told you your son was going to be a wild animal of a man and was going to fight with everyone, including his own family? Would you respond like Hagar and say, "Truly here I have seen him who looks after me"?[5] Consider the following:

- The angel begins with the promise of multiplying Hagar's offspring,

- instructs her to name the child Ishmael (God will hear) because "the LORD has listened to your affliction," and

- Hagar's response is positive.

All this suggests that our interaction with verse 12 is a censored kiss and there's something we're missing. The element of verse 12 that David *unveiled* is the imagery of Ishmael's "hand against everyone and everyone's hand against him." The mental picture is that of two fists colliding, especially as it follows "wild donkey of a man" and concludes with "shall dwell over against his kinsmen." The conclusion that there is an aggressive and contentious connotation is virtually unavoidable. But the image that David presented was not two fists colliding but rather two hands embracing each other, more like a handshake. The phrase "he's got his hands in everything" would be an accurate comparison from modern American English vernacular.

The word translated "wild donkey" is *pereh* and finds its root in the Hebrew word *paw-raw'* which means "to bear fruit." Fruitfulness is clearly indicated in verse 10 of chapter 16 when Hagar is told, "I will surely multiply your offspring," and later echoed in Genesis 17:20, "As for Ishmael, I have heard you [Abraham]; behold, *I have blessed him and will make him fruitful and multiply him greatly*" (emphasis added). It's clear that Ishmael is blessed by God and not cursed. This word *pereh* is found several times in Scripture,[6] and is consistently translated into some variation of "wild donkey," with a specific relation to an Asian donkey known as an "onager." The onager is native to Southwest Asia and benefits from a lower center of gravity and horselike strength, attributes making it well suited for its environment and valuable in domesticated capacities. The onager, however, is commonly recognized as untamed.[7] The book of Job uses *pereh* multiple times, and for our purposes we'll examine the following:

> "Who has let the wild donkey go free? Who has loosed the bonds of the swift donkey, to whom I have given the arid plain for his home and the salt land for his dwelling place? He scorns the tumult of the city; he hears not the shouts of the driver. He ranges the mountains as his pasture, and he searches after every green thing. (Job 39:5–8)

Returning to Genesis 16:12, the final words of the verse state, "[Ishmael] shall dwell over against all his brethren." When examined in the Hebrew, this also agrees with the premise that this prophecy concerning Ishmael is, in fact, a blessing and not a curse. Even today, Middle Eastern cultures value community, and tribal identity is esteemed above the individual. In the ancient world this was certainly the case. For someone to be separated from his *kinsmen* was shameful. For Ishmael to dwell with his kinsmen was also a blessing. Other translations demonstrate that the Hebrew is speaking about Ishmael's being *with* his kinsmen, not in *contention* with them: the King James translations says, "in the presence of"; the Young Literal Translation says, "before the face of."

Taken together, we could translate this verse to say, "He will be fruitful, well adapted to his environment, and unburdened, with none to oppress him; his hand will be involved in everything, and he will dwell in the presence of his kinsmen."

That agrees with Hagar's response and the Lord's affirmation of *blessing* upon Ishmael in Genesis 17:20.[8] Unfortunately, in some cases, the translation isn't just a bad kiss—it's a slap in the face! Here's what the New Living Translation does with Genesis 16:20:

> "This son of yours will be a wild man, as untamed as a wild donkey! He will raise his fist against everyone, and everyone will be against him. Yes, he will live in open hostility against all his relatives."

You don't have to be theologian to understand that those words don't qualify as a blessing! If you'd been Hagar and heard those words, there's no chance that you would have responded with, "Truly here I have seen him who looks after me." Hagar responded the way she did because what she heard was a blessing and not a curse. The meaning of the words discussed above are not without debate, however, Hagar's response evidence the intentions of a Heavenly Father. Hagar encountered a God who heard her and comforted her in her affliction, a God who intervened and got involved in the mess that was being made. He reached down to broken and hurting humanity and once again put His hands in the dirt!

It's important for us to consider the consequences of how the traditional hermeneutic of this verse is understood and how it influences our perception of the Arab world. Take, for example, the footnote found in the Amplified Bible in accordance with the word "wild" in Genesis 16:12:

> Nothing can be more descriptive of the wandering, lawless, freebooting life of the Arabs than this. From the beginning

to the present they have kept their independence, and God preserves them as a lasting monument of His providential care and an incontestable argument of the truth of divine revelation. Had the books of Moses no other proof of their divine origin, the account of Ishmael and the prophecy concerning his descendants during a period of nearly 4,000 years would be sufficient. To attempt to refute it would be a ridiculous presumption and folly. (Adam Clarke, *The Holy Bible with a Commentary*).[9]

The strength of Clarke's language is evidence enough of why many have fallen in this ditch of hermeneutic error and either consciously or subconsciously considered the Arabs a cursed people. Essentially, commentaries such as Clarke's tells us that God cursed a slave woman and her unborn child when her only conceivable fault was running away from an abusive mistress. Rendering the text this way is tantamount to accusing God of having multiple personalities and stripping Him of His immutable character. I would argue that this hermeneutic is the diseased fruit of supercessionism, which has found room for itself in the space created by the false dichotomy between the Old and the New Testament. If Israel and the Jewish people can be replaced, surely Ishmael's promise and purpose can be replaced with a judgment and a curse. This infection can be remedied, and it must, lest the church keep the Arab people from actualizing their destiny and God's intended blessing.

I told you right from the start I was going to invite you to think. We've reached an important point of the story, and it's time to connect some dots.

- God's ultimate agenda is to glorify Himself and bring all people to the saving knowledge of God.

- The Abrahamic covenant reveals the plan for this ultimate agenda; it is an eternal and unconditional covenant with the inextricable elements of *land* and *people.*

- Powers and principalities (evil forces in heavenly places) are at work, influencing people contrary to God's ultimate agenda. They are created beings lacking imagination or innovation.

- Value and purpose are not synonymous or equivalent. Having a specific purpose (irrevocable gift or calling) does not dictate value, but rather serves to clarify purpose.

Therefore, the only strategies that powers and principalities can employ will either oppose the revealed purposes of God or create a counterfeit. First, we'll look at an authentic purpose and then follow with the counterfeit.

In Genesis 17 God does two things: (1) identifies Isaac as the promised heir of the Abrahamic covenant and (2) confirms His blessing to Ishmael (see Gen. 17:19–20). Through faith in and identification with Jesus, those of us without Jewish lineage are counted as "sons of Abraham" (Gal. 3:7). This is valid and efficacious due to Jesus' death and resurrection. The promise to Abraham became a covenant, and it was ratified in successive generations. It is eternal and unconditional. The promise to Ishmael was not a covenant, it was not ratified to successive generations, and while the promise was in fact fulfilled, it has no eternal quality. God's promise to Abraham is consequential for all mankind; the promise to Ishmael is only consequential for Ishmael.

FALSE NARRATIVE AND FALSE HOPE

Now for the counterfeit: through a religious ideology (Islam) a false narrative places Ishmael as the promised heir of Abraham (literally replacing Isaac with Ishmael at the binding on Moriah in Genesis 22) and propagates identification with Ishmael while not having legitimate genealogical ties. It's a false story and a false faith leading to a false hope and spiritual bondage.

The intensity and scope (demographically and geographically) of Islam's influence over the Arab world is evidence of God's intended redemptive purpose for the Arab world. The prophetic potential of the Arab people is in direct correlation with the activity of powers and principalities.

While cosmic powers contending against God's purposes have failed to bring about Israel's destruction, they have succeed in their efforts of deception. As we saw earlier, those seeds of deception have taken root in the church, and our attention now is on how that deception has overtaken a people with outrageous redemptive purpose: the Arabs. No other Gentile people group on the planet has greater potential to "make Israel jealous" than the Arabs, especially the Palestinians.

Islam's founder, Muhammad (an Arab from Arabia) claimed to be a descendant of Ishmael. Islam, as it spread, also Arabized the people it conquered and through a false narrative empowered a counterfeit patriarch in Ishmael. The origin of and current concentration of Islam finds itself geographically surrounding both elements of the Abrahamic covenant (the land and the people). And the overwhelming majority of the Arab world is held captive by Islamic religious ideologies that are at odds with those covenantal elements. To call this a coincidence is a harder sell than the convergence of the largest mosque in

North America and Henry Ford's backyard. While we're on the topic of *coincidence*, we should mention one of Henry Ford's admirers: Adolf Hitler.

Hitler praised Henry Ford in *Mein Kampf:* "It is Jews who govern the Stock Exchange forces of the American union. Every year makes them more and more the controlling masters of the producers in a nation of one hundred and twenty millions; only a single great man, Ford, to their fury, still maintains full independence."[10] Not only did Hitler specifically praise Henry Ford in *Mein Kampf,* but many of Hitler's ideas were also a direct reflection of Ford's racist philosophy. There is a great similarity between *The International Jew* and Hitler's *Mein Kampf,* and some passages are so identical that it has been said Hitler copied directly from Ford's publication. Hitler also read Ford's autobiography, *My Life and Work* (which was published in 1922 and was a best seller in Germany) as well as Ford's book *Today and Tomorrow.* There can be no doubt as to the influence of Henry Ford's ideas on Hitler.[11]

The vitriol revitalized by Ford finds its origins farther down the corridors of history than Russian czars and the *Protocols of the Elders of Zion.* This animosity against the land and the people of covenant goes back in antiquity to Haman[12] (Esther 3:8–9) and Pharaoh (Ex. 1:9–22). Hitler, in his time, clearly expressed his views of the Jewish endeavor to return to their ancestral homeland:

> For while the Zionists try to make the rest of the world believe that the national consciousness of the Jew finds it satisfaction in the creation of a Palestinian state, the Jews again slyly dupe the dumb *goyim* [Yiddish for Gentiles]. It

doesn't even enter their heads to build up a Jewish state in Palestine for the purpose of living there; all they want is a central organization for their international world swindle, endowed with its own sovereign rights and removed from the intervention of other states: a haven for convicted scoundrels and a university for budding crooks.[13]

In addition to Ford, Hitler had other *coincidental* alliances along his path to the "Final Solution": Saudi royal counselor Khalid al Hud, and Sayid Amin al Husseini, the grand mufti of Jerusalem, the supreme Islamic authority in Palestine.

One June 17, Hitler received the Saudi Royal Counselor Khalid Al Hud, sent as special envoy by King Ibn Saud, for a lengthy consultation at the Obersalzberg. After the talk, Hitler asked the emissary to join him and his entourage for tea. (June 12, 1939)[14]

Part of Hitler's discussion with the Saudi ambassador on June 12, 1939:

[We have sympathy for the Arabs] because we were jointly fighting the Jews. This led him to discuss Palestine and conditions there, and he then stated that he himself would not rest until the last Jew had left Germany. Kalid al Hud observed that the Prophet Mohammed . . . had acted the same way. He had driven the Jews out of Arabia.[15]

Hitler returned to Berlin the next morning. On the same day, he received the Grand Mufti of Jerusalem at the Reich Chancellery "for a discussion of great importance." . . . "In the presence of Reich Foreign Minister von Ribbentrop, the Führer received the Grand Mufti of Palestine, Sayid Amin al Husseini, for a heartfelt discussion of great importance for the future of the Arab countries."[16]

On July 15, he received the former prime minister of Iraq, Rashid Ali al Gailani, who had so pitifully failed the previous year and had then emigrated. This sad figure fitted in perfectly well with Hitler's other foreign guests, especially the Grand Mufti of Jerusalem . . . "The Führer received the Iraqi Prime Minister Rashid Ali al Gailani on Wednesday [July 15] in the presence of Reich Foreign Minister von Ribbentrop. The discussion took place in the spirit of the trusting friendship that the German Volk feels for the Arab people."[17]

Hitler allied with Amin al-Husseini, the infamously anti-Semitic mufti, and the two plotted the global annihilation of the Jewish people.[18] Hitler and Muslims not only shared views regarding the Jews; they also shared views about Christians. Germany was a Christian nation,[19] and Christians in Nazi Germany were considered Aryan. Those who aligned with the Nazi political agenda and didn't oppose Hitler's "Final Solution" were not at risk. Europe was predominantly Christian, and Hitler used the writings of Martin Luther, a Christian German national hero, to justify his xenophobia and genocidal agenda. See the following example taken from a speech Hitler gave shortly after being released from prison:

> Martin Luther has been the greatest encouragement of my life. Luther was a great man. He was a giant. With one blow he heralded the coming of the new dawn and the new age. He saw clearly that the Jews need to be destroyed, and we're only beginning to see that we need to carry this work on . . . I believe that today I am acting in accordance with the will of Almighty God as I announce the most important work

that Christians could undertake—and that is to be against the Jews and get rid of them once and for all.[20]

When it served his purposes, he invoked the anti-Semitic writings of Luther and presented a theological justification of his actions. However, by his own admission, Hitler had disdain for Christianity:

> You see, it's been our misfortune to have the wrong religion. Why didn't we have the religion of the Japanese, who regard sacrifice for the Fatherland as the highest good? The Mohammedan religion too would have been much more compatible to us than Christianity. Why did it have to be Christianity with its meekness and flabbiness?[21]

Christians in Muslim-majority lands have a comparable experience in regard to political alliances. The current pressure placed on Palestinian Christians to align with the political agenda (fueled by a religious and vehemently anti-Semitic ideology) of the Palestinian Authority has roots that reach much deeper than Hitler and al-Husseini. It touches the very inception of Islam.

The rise of the Islamic State in Iraq and Syria (ISIS) warrants the world's attention and requires appropriate action. Media coverage of ISIS has introduced the Western world to an Islamic concept foreign to most non-Muslims: *jizya*. Non-Muslim populations subjugated by the violent colonization of Islam (jihad) had to "recognize Islamic ownership of their land, submit to Islamic law, and accept payment of the poll tax (*jizya*)."[22] This tax was part of a sociopolitical status imposed on indigenous non-Muslim peoples conquered by jihad. *Dhimmitude* follows jihad.[23] This practice was applied to the People of the Book (Book = Bible; thus referring primarily to Jews and Christians);[24] it goes back to the eighth century, and it is very Islamic.

Trying to understand Middle Eastern Christianity without appreciating the effects of generations of dhimmitude is like trying to understand American culture without knowing anything about college sports, Thanksgiving, or democracy! The identity of the Arab Christian community, regardless of denomination or tradition, is deeply influenced by centuries of surviving among a Muslim majority.

THE DETAILS ARE IN THE DEED

Now that we've taken a moment to consider the bigger picture, let's examine the pieces of the puzzle. What we'll find is that dhimmitude is not only represented in extremes, such as ISIS, it's pervasive throughout the Muslim world. One example will introduce a Palestinian Christian farmer, Daoud Nasser.

Daoud owns a parcel of land in the West Bank, south of Bethlehem, that Israel declared state land in the early 1990s. The land has been in his family since the days of World War I. He has been in litigation ever since then in order to keep it and has dubbed the parcel the "Tent of Nations," a place where "people build bridges." It has since become a regular tourist attraction for a number of Christian groups, particularly those funded by George Soros and other left-wing interest groups.

By way of preliminaries, it is important to note that, on the surface, Daoud is doing some good things: he runs children's camps, and in many ways exhibits an outwardly congenial and benevolent personality, all of which I have seen with my own eyes.

However, based on the research I have done, including

visiting the land and interviewing Daoud himself, his claims are simply untenable; and the way in which the "Tent of Nations" has been used to delegitimize Israel is entirely unjustified.

First, Daoud claims that the land is his because he has a "deed" to it. This is true; he does have a deed. But there is an extremely important caveat: not all deeds are the same. Just because someone has a deed does not mean he owns a piece of property outright. In American law, there are many types of estates that can be transferred by a deed, and only one of them vests full and absolute ownership in the person to whom the deed is conveyed.

Daoud's family obtained a deed to the land in the early twentieth century under the Ottoman Empire. The details of all the legalities can be reduced to this: Ottoman law had five categories of land ownership. Those relevant to this case are *mulk* and *miri*. *Mulk* land was full private ownership (full title), what in American law is called a "fee simple absolute." *Miri* land, on the other hand, was only partial title. Under a *miri* deed, title remained with the sultan/state who had the right to reclaim the land if it was not cultivated for any three-year period. The idea behind *miri* land was that the government wanted it to remain cultivated and productive and thereby provide tax revenue. If it weren't used accordingly, the government would reclaim the land and auction it off to someone else who would make it productive.

So what kind of deed did Daoud's family obtain? According to a very pro-Daoud BBC article, he obtained a *miri* deed. The article never stated this, but the writer included a picture of one of the original deeds. Sure enough, it was classified not as *mulk* (full private ownership), but as *miri*, which is only partial (and revocable) ownership.

Thus, under their *miri* deed, Daoud's family never had full title to the land, and the government had every right to reclaim it if it was not cultivated for any three-year period. As it turns out, Daoud's land was not cultivated for a number of years (far more than three), which is proven by numerous satellite photos taken in the 1980s, 1990s, and 2000s.

Therefore, Israel, as the state in effective control of the West Bank after the Six-Day War of 1967, and applying the law under which the deed was originally conveyed and was applied by both the British and Jordanian occupiers of the West Bank before 1967, had the right under the terms of the deed and according to the legal property interests it conveyed to reclaim the land as "state land."

Near Daoud's land, there is a famous Israeli settlement named Efrat. I visited with one of its residents who showed me a sizable piece of land that divided two portions of the settlement. It was beautiful and contained a gorgeous and fruitful vineyard. Sure enough, this land belonged to a Palestinian. And though it would be ideal for the further expansion of Efrat, the Israeli government, and the residents of Efrat themselves, do not touch it. In fact, relations between the Palestinian and his Israeli neighbors are good. The reason for this is simple: the Palestinian farmer has proven that he, in fact, does own the land (a fact that, as happens frequently in a part of the world that has been slow to adopt a uniform and written form of land registration, can be quite difficult to prove).

Second, Daoud claims that he is being oppressed by the evil occupier, Israel, and that he simply wants Israel to see him as a human being. He frequently appeals to evangelical Christians, claiming that despite being oppressed, he loves his enemy anyway. This all sounds quite noble until one actually digs into the facts.

Does an evil occupier

1. go through nearly twenty-five years of litigation to get a piece of land, or do they simply take it?

2. allow a case by those they occupy to go to their nation's Supreme Court?

3. allow the occupied, against the greater weight of the evidence, to reregister their land under Israeli law (as Israel has now done for Daoud), and thus better secure the rights of a Palestinian farmer to that land?

Such was the conduct of the "evil occupier" in this case.

Since the land has not been surveyed in more than five years, Daoud must have a survey done in order to reregister it, a process that will cost him about ten thousand dollars. But land surveys are expensive everywhere, including the United States. So Daoud can hardly claim that the expense, or the fact that the survey is required, is unique to Israel or the result of the "occupation." This is a normal feature of property law in every civilized portion of the globe.

Daoud frequently points to the fact that the Israeli Army bulldozed approximately fifteen hundred trees on "his" land a few years ago. Again, the problem with this claim is not that it is false, but that it has been disingenuously de-contextualized: this land was in dispute, and it was going through litigation. Israel declared it state land, and the matter was being resolved. As it turns out, it was never Daoud's land to do with as he wished from the very beginning (per his deed). Daoud planted on it anyway. Israel has engaged in the exact same actions when it came to illegally built Jewish settlements, outposts, and other buildings in the West Bank that lacked the proper permits. An example is the Migron settlement in 2012, in which Israel expelled hundreds of settlers who had illegally built on private Palestinian land.

At the same time, if Daoud were to sell his land to Israel, or give it up in any way, he would likely be in the crosshairs of the Palestinian Authority, which has made it illegal, under penalty of death, to sell or transfer "Palestinian land" to Israel, or to any Jew whatsoever.

This, for both Daoud himself and those Christians who naively and without any critical eye whatsoever accept such anti-Israel propaganda at face value, begs the question: who is it that *actually* sees Daoud as less than a human being—Israel, or his own fellow Palestinians?

Israel is the only place in the Middle East where Christian communities are free to worship and grow. Arab–Israeli Christians have a quality of life and a freedom of religious expression unparalleled by any other Middle Eastern country. An Arab–Israeli Christian sits on Israel's supreme court; other religious minorities, such as the Druze, have high-ranking positions in the military and in Israel's Ministry of Foreign Affairs.

Magda Manosur, the Israeli-Druze woman mentioned earlier, shared something very precious with me during one of our visits together: her teenage son dreams of serving in an elite combat unit of the Israeli Defense Force (IDF). Friends, if Israel is an oppressive, discriminatory, apartheid country, why in the world would a little Druze boy dream of becoming his oppressor? The answer is quite simple: he's not oppressed! At the time of this writing, the IDF has a record-breaking level of Arab–Israeli Christian recruits.[25]

On the contrary, the Christian community in the Gaza Strip, under the rule of the terrorist organization Hamas, has almost vanished entirely.[26] Under the West Bank's "moderate" Palestinian Authority, Christians such as Pastor Naim Khoury literally risk their lives by transgressing the status quo established by a Muslim majority rule guided by the Islamic ideology of dhimmitude. Pastor Khoury's situation is augmented by his theology regarding Israel. His belief in and teaching of the Old Testament is his greatest deviation from the status quo and the most dangerous.

Palestinians who are actively in favor of or affiliated with Israel in way that does not perpetuate the Palestinian political agenda or narrative are viewed as "collaborators," be they Christian or Muslim. These collaborators often pay with their lives. In Gaza, the body of an alleged collaborator was chained to a motorcycle and dragged through the main streets.[27] In 1970 a group was founded to protect Yasir Arafat and other elite PLO personnel. In addition to security, this group, Force 17, conducted counterterrorist service against internal rivals and collaborators; in particular, against those involved in the sale of land to Israelis.[28]

Most of our attention has been focused on the dynamics between metanarrative and sub-narratives: *the* story, how it relates to *our* story, and vice versa. Several years ago a conversation with a Palestinian friend from Bethlehem alerted me to another layer of complexity: dual narratives. Our conversation took a political tone, and it wasn't long before I realized that we had two different accounts of modern history. I began to ask some questions about historic fact, elements of the Arab–Israeli conflict that are well documented and uncontested. He believed a fabricated narrative. Because he is an Arabic-speaker, his exposure to information about the conflict is almost exclusively in Arabic, and what I learned that day is that much of it is revisionist history.

"WHAT I SAW WAS A PARADISE"

On my first trip to Israel, we took an excursion to Bethlehem, which is under the complete control of the Palestinian Authority and lies behind the security barrier erected during the second intifada. We saw the typical tourist locations and ended the day at a great restaurant with an amazing view overlooking the "Shepherds' Field," where it is said the angels announced Jesus' birth to the shepherds. Naturally, the restaurant was managed by Palestinians, and our waiter was a young Palestinian man. Not only was the food excellent, but the service was impeccable.

So I thought to myself (not knowing I would go on to visit Israel many times), I could possibly never be in Bethlehem again, and this could be my only chance to actually get to hear the perspective of Palestinians. Why not ask them some questions?

So I called to my waiter (we'll call him "Ali" for the sake of his safety), and said "Hey, Ali, come over here real quick."

"Yes, sir, what may I do for you, sir?"

"Ali, what do you think of Israel?"

Suddenly, all conversation at the table stopped, my dinner companions fell silent, and I could sense that they truly were afraid of what might come next. Everyone knew I was the guy who asked a lot of questions, but they probably didn't think I would go that far.

But what came next surprised everyone: we actually had a

great conversation. Ali explained that Israel was his "enemy," and that he has a right to what he called "my land," which Israel is denying him. But then he went on to say something I found chilling:

"The truth is, Josh, Palestinians don't want peace."

I didn't quite know how to respond to that except to ask him to explain, which he did, listing the typical list of Palestinian grievances against Israel.

However, Ali and I liked each other. Our conversation never became heated. My goal was to simply listen and learn. I was not there to debate this young man, or any Palestinian. In a way, I didn't feel that I, a first-time visiting Christian from America, had any right to tell this man how he should feel, despite my beliefs about the conflict. He lived it day in, day out. I did not. I was going back home to a rather comfortable existence in a few days. He would continue to remain here.

So Ali and I exchanged phone numbers and e-mails. We would go on to become good friends, communicating frequently, and exchanging a great deal of conversation.

Then we had a conversation maybe six months after I returned that stunned me. We had not talked in maybe a month, so we were catching up. But Ali was not the same person I had met six months earlier. His outlook on the conflict had totally changed. Inwardly, he told me, he had been really struggling with his former convictions about the "evil occupier."

It all started when his father was arrested by the Palestinian Authority. He used to work in their department of labor, but he did not toe the line when it came to the PA's rabid anti-Semitism and rampant corruption. Despite the fact that he was highly educated, experienced, and good at his job, he was thrown in jail for a few weeks. What opened Ali's eyes is how his father was treated while in the captivity of his own people, fellow Palestinians. His father was a diabetic, and yet there was zero effort made to secure him any insulin. While in prison, he was hardly fed, and the conditions were absolutely miserable. No one attempted to alleviate his condition whatsoever. There was no due process of law, only protestations about how he would be indefinitely detained.

What happened to Ali's father is far too common in the Palestinian-controlled territories. The Independent Commission of Human Rights (ICHR) 2014 report, *The Status of Human Rights in Palestine*, records the deaths of Palestinians in Palestinian prisons and detention centers in the Gaza Strip and believes the detainees were subjected to extrajudicial executions.[29] The report includes complaints of arbitrary detention, torture, disregard for court rulings, violations of the right of peaceful assembly, and "lawlessness" in the Gaza Strip.

Eventually he was released, but Ali's eyes had been opened. He had seen this sort of thing happen to others, but he just assumed they were traitors. Now it had happened to his own father. And what made it all the more powerful was this: his father had been previously imprisoned by the Israelis. And how had they treated him? He slept comfortably, was fed plenty of food, and he was provided with insulin for his diabetes. Ali was beginning to have his view of Israel rocked.

"My own people treats us like dogs, but my enemy at least treats me like a human being."

The young, angry, hate-filled Palestinian man I had met was undergoing a radical transformation. He had seen the symptoms of the problem for years but had never fully connected the dots.

"The truth is, Josh," he told me over the phone, "we [the Palestinians] don't deserve this land. Look at the Jews: they have their own problems, and they don't do everything perfectly, but they at least work together. They *love* each other. Palestinians do not love their fellow Palestinians. If you speak your mind, you could be thrown in jail or killed. If someone dies, people bury them apathetically but never ask you how you are doing, or extend a helping hand. Our own government treats us like dogs."

He continued: "This became clearer to me, Josh, not only when I saw how differently the Israelis treated my father as compared to my own people, but when I was allowed to visit Israel itself. They gave me a pass to come to Jerusalem to celebrate Ramadan. What I saw was a *paradise*. Living under the Israeli government was a *paradise* compared to living under the Palestinian Authority. People could say what they wanted; they could do what they wanted; they could worship how they wanted . . . including me! But when I returned to my own people and my own government, all those things were instantly stripped from me."

And then came the statement that shocked me perhaps the most: "Josh, I would much rather be a citizen of Israel. *The Jews deserve this land*, not because of religion or anything like that, but because they love each other, and because they treat me like a human being. Even when my father had issues with the Israeli authorities, there was rule of law. He went to a court, he could appeal his case and, while in prison, he was treated like a human being. I never had to worry that my father would be mistreated when he was in an Israeli jail. But I didn't know if he would come out alive after being in a Palestinian jail."

One can only imagine my shock upon hearing these things. I was arranging another trip to Israel, Jordan, and Egypt to research for this book. Ali and I were able to set up some time for me to spend with him and his family in their refugee camp (which I will not name for security reasons). His family was an exceptionally generous, hospitable, and loving Muslim family. His father recounted the stories Ali had told me himself. He could barely walk, and his diabetes had affected the circulation to his legs. But he was a man of great honor and integrity.

Ali's father had more things to tell my team and me that would further surprise us. "Before the second intifada," he said, "there was complete freedom of movement for Palestinians and Israelis. Everyone could go wherever they wanted: Gaza, the West Bank, and Israel proper. Israelis could shop in Gaza, and Palestinians could shop in Tel Aviv. Could you imagine such a thing today?" Indeed, we couldn't. As we spoke, Gaza was under the iron fist of Hamas (which happened after the unilateral Israeli withdrawal from Gaza in 2005), and the security barrier had gone up to protect Israeli civilians from the massive waves of suicide bombings that occurred during the second intifada in the early 2000s.

"Not only that, but many Palestinians were making a lot more money. Israeli companies could operate freely in Gaza and the West Bank, and Palestinians could work in Israel. That's how we were able to afford this nice home [he gestured around his living room]. Life was a lot better for many Palestinians before the Palestinian Authority, and certainly before the intifada."

During that research trip, I found beautiful, wonderful, educated, and highly intelligent people on all sides. I can no longer lump the whole Middle East, and certainly not all Muslims, into one nice box. Truth be told, in both Jordan and Egypt, I found that I was liked for simply being American, even when I wasn't handing out money. I thought there would be some sort of smoldering dislike, but there was none. Quite the opposite, in fact, even in Palestinian cities.

At the same time, I ran into some extremely disturbing things as well. The questions naturally arise: Why is this happening? Why are Israel and the Palestinians still fighting? Is peace even possible anymore? The answers to these questions are both extremely complex and exceedingly simple.

Here is a preliminary fact that must be acknowledged: what we are seeing on our screens are not isolated events. A friend of mine recently observed that human nature prefers to think of history as beginning at our own births and contingent upon our own experiences. This is very true, particularly for the Israeli/Palestinian conflict. History did not begin with a killed or wounded Palestinian; neither did it begin with Israel retaliating for some rockets being fired at their cities. History did not begin with the images we see in the media today or with a sob story everyone is tweeting or sharing on Facebook, of which there are many on both sides.

So why is this happening? All things being equal, it boils down to the utter unwillingness of Arab leadership ever to accept a Jewish state in any territory ever under the sovereignty of the Dar al-Islam ("House of Islam"). Decades before anything we are seeing on our screens happened, the leaders of the Arab Palestinians were instigating massacres of Jews (1929 riots, 1937 massacres, etc.) before Israel even existed, and they even worked with Hitler in implementing the Holocaust. The UN partitioned a truncated Palestine Mandate into an Arab and Jewish state (in contravention of the original League of Nations mandate), and even though it included virtually none of

Judaism's holiest sites (including Jerusalem), the Jews accepted it, and the Arabs did not.

The surrounding Arab nations then initiated a genocidal campaign to annihilate Israel upon its declaration of independence in 1948. Before Israel ever occupied the West Bank in 1967, terrorist attacks against it were relatively commonplace. The PLO was founded on the principle of destroying Israel. Fatah was founded on the same principle. Hamas also, and the leadership of the PA has pursued the same course. Don't believe me? Read their words. Read their documents. It's there for all to see. But of course, such archives are neither sexy nor bloody enough for the headlines. The Palestinians have been offered nearly all of the West Bank, East Jerusalem, and a limited repatriation of the so-called refugees of 1948 ("so-called" because they are largely the descendants of those refugees, not the refugees themselves). These offers came as recently as 2000 under Prime Minister Barak and 2008 under Prime Minister Olmert. Both were refused. Why? Because the leadership (contrary to the desires of many ordinary Palestinians) are not interested in a Palestinian state. They are far more interested in the destruction of the one Jewish state, whose right to exist they still refuse to acknowledge.

So why are they still fighting? Again, a long, complicated answer is really quite necessary, but here is what I experienced when visiting with Palestinian leaders while conducting my research: They live in a historical la-la land. They have made it up as they go, and they indoctrinate their people with fraudulent myths about utterly basic and incontrovertible facts of history.

I was told several absolutely outrageous things: the Arab nations did *not* invade Israel in 1948; the Jews made it up. The PA is the only true democracy in the Middle East (a laugh, to be sure, as Ali and his father well knew). Muslims lived at *complete* peace with the Jews before 1948, and Jews were absolutely equal with Muslims in the Arab countries from which they fled to Israel in 1948 (equality can be quite nerve-racking, after all). The Palestinians have *never* made a mistake . . . ever! Even the patriotic Israeli leaders I met with all had critiques of their country. One official in the Ministry of Foreign Affairs even told me, "I think we get it right only 75 percent of the time." Look at the Knesset, which has Arabs, Muslims, and Jews: you'll see rambunctious debate on the screen constantly, and Israeli civil society is full of self-criticism and debate.

But it continued to get worse with the Palestinian leaders. One was even trying to convince me of how peaceful his intentions were. When I brought up suicide bombings against civilians, however, he literally said, "I don't support suicide bombing, but I don't condemn it either." And apparently Israel is in control of Europe and America—completely. They were positive. One of the men who told me these things was educated at a top American university and served as the mayor of a Palestinian town. Another was a very smart, prominent businessman. Yet another was a longtime member of Fatah. They treated us very well, but to say they were brainwashed would be tame. These were not matters of deep discussion and debate—they were utterly basic facts being rejected in favor of myths. It was like being told with a straight face that the pope was Muslim. The member of Fatah compared what was happening to Palestinians to the Holocaust. And yet, I don't remember ever hearing about Jews in the Holocaust eating big meals (as we had just done), meeting with friends freely (as these Palestinians had just done), having nice smartphones (as all of them had), and being able to go about and do their business as they saw fit (as they all did). Somehow when I spent time in Bethlehem, I didn't get the sense I was in Auschwitz and, unlike Bethlehem, neither did Auschwitz ever have thousands of tourists every year when it was functioning.

ARAB-ISRAELI CONFLICT SYNDROME

There is a disturbing phenomenon afoot, and it is the growing number of Christians who believe the often-vitriolic, anti-Israel propaganda that has become so common in our day.

That is not to say that Israel is never at fault. Israel is in many ways a nation like any other. Neither is it to say that believing such propaganda makes one anti-Semitic by default.

It *does* mean that, very sadly, more and more Christians are partaking of what I have called the "Arab–Israeli conflict syndrome," a condition characterized by people feeling entitled to have very strong opinions and feelings on a conflict they know exceptionally little about and for which historical context and complexities are so crucial to understand.[30] The result is too often taking headlines and ginned-up stories far more seriously than they deserve, and the delegitimization of the one and only Jewish state in an unjust manner. Sandra Teplinsky, president of Light of Zion (an outreach to Israel), speaks to this issue in her excellent book *Why Still Care About Israel?*

> Lacking objective documentation of their plight, Palestinians have amassed global sympathies through a narrative that inverts history. Many share tragic personal tales that prove either unverifiable or outrageously embellished. Their stories tend either to romanticize Arab tribal-village life or misrepresent

it as a bustling society. Sadly, some of these accounts are presented by Christians as honest-to-God facts. Their pitiable tales tug at the heartstrings of any hearer. *It's their personal story*, we reason. *How can it not be true—and how can we not be deeply moved?* Emotions are stirred, then inflamed against Israel. Gradually, hearts are hardened against the Jewish people and what God is doing with them today.[31]

I dealt with this embellishment and false narrative in an acute way with a young American who had spent several months living in the West Bank. She had all the symptoms of the Arab–Israeli conflict syndrome. With a sincere love for Jesus and the Palestinians, she volunteered in a Christian school, and as one would imagine, she cultivated a deep affection for the Palestinian people, an affection I share with her. Over the course of a few weeks of traveling through Israel with a group of students, I had the opportunity to correct misinformation and provide context that allowed her to see the big picture. She had mistakenly confused agreement with the narrative she was presented by her Palestinian hosts with her love for them. For her to come to a different conclusion than what she had been told by *Palestinian Christians* felt like betrayal. Emotionally, after months of growing to love the children and families she served, it was much easier to maintain their narrative—romanticize biblical Israel, and vilify modern Israel.

With watery eyes she approached me with her most troubling issue, one which apparently had been her Palestinian hosts' most troubling issue: "What about the settlements?" she asked, almost hoping the tension of the dual narratives would be eased by an inadequate response. While settlements are by no means a nonissue, they're not the main issue. The problem is not the presence of settlements; the problem is what happened when they weren't there. Between 1949 and 1967, when Judea and Samaria (West Bank) were occupied by Jordan following the Independence War, there was no push for a Palestinian State, and Arab aggression against Israel continued despite the absence of Jewish communities. In 1948 the UN sent Count Folke Bernadotte to negotiate a truce during the War of Independence. In his diary he wrote:

> The Palestinian Arabs had at present no will of their own. Neither have they ever developed any specifically Palestinian nationalism. The demand for a separate Arab state in Palestine is consequently relatively weak. It would seem as though in existing circumstances most of the Palestinian Arabs would be quite content to be incorporated in Transjordan.[32]

After 1967, when the Six-Day War brought an end to the Jordanian occupation, the resultant presence of Jewish communities (settlements) in Judea and Samaria (West Bank) had dramatic consequences for Palestinians. From 1969 to 1979, under Israeli management, the West Bank and Gaza comprised one of the "most dynamic economies on the earth, with a decade of growth at a rate of 30 percent per year."[33] The Arab population rose from 1 million to 3 million while the Jewish population rose to 250,000; per-capita income tripled in the West Bank and Gaza; the economy boomed with little foreign aid; Palestinian workers in Israel went from 0 to 109,000 by 1986; life expectancy rose from forty-eight in 1967 to seventy-two in 2000. By 1986, 92.8 percent of the population had electricity around the clock, as compared to 20.5 percent in 1967.[34] It would seem that the same Jewish people that made a matchless contribution to the world, congruent with their history and God's covenant, were now *blessing* the Palestinians.

Jewish immigration during the First, Second, and Third Aliyah had a similar effect on the local population. Before World War I, Arabic speakers were emigrating from the region of Palestine. Between World War I and World War II, as the Jewish population increased, the Arab population increased by 120 percent;[35] 37 percent of that growth was due to Arab immigration from neighboring states by those who wanted to take advantage of the higher standard of living made possible by the Jews.[36] Jews drained the malarial swamps and brought improved sanitation and health care, lowering the infant mortality rate from 201 per thousand in 1925 to 94 per thousand in 1945; and life expectancy rose from thirty-seven years in 1926 to forty-nine in 1943.[37]

While conducting my interviews in preparation for this book, I asked Israelis and Palestinians, "What would you do differently?" Each Israeli I asked readily responded, identifying both mistakes Israel has made and things that Israel should have done differently, or not at all. When I asked this of Palestinians, the consistent response to the same question was, "Nothing," followed by a justification of everything Palestinians have done. Some even justified suicide bombings.

The combination of a fabricated narrative and the absence of self-criticism are paralyzing efforts to find a solution to the conflict. Again, I want to acknowledge that my intention is not to whitewash Israel. Israel, like other nations, is far from perfect. However, in many ways she is unlike other nations (especially Middle Eastern ones), and those differences, as noted in chapter

5, are exemplary. Unlike the Arab nations and their attempts to annihilate the Jewish people, Israel has never had a genocidal motivation in dealing with the Palestinians. The Jewish contribution to humanity, modern Israel's perpetual innovation (from computers to water conservation), and its position as the lone democracy in the Middle East are not indicators of a malevolent, genocidal entity. Perhaps the strongest evidence of this is Israel's diplomatic relations with Germany. Israel can be amicable with a nation who systemically murdered 6 million Jews, and yet reconciliation with Palestinians is so elusive.

Reconciliation is a relational process, and relationship is the currency of the kingdom of God. Few people I know understand how relationships facilitate the purpose of God as well as Bishop Roberts Stearns, the founder and executive director of Eagles' Wings. Earlier I mentioned David Nekrutman and Pastor Naim Khoury. Over the years I have become friends with David and Pastor Naim as well as Pastor Steven Khoury, Naim's son. David and Steven have also become friends, and this unorthodox relationship between an Orthodox Jew and a Palestinian Christian began at a birthday party. Bishop Stearns introduced David and Steven, and a friendship was forged. David and Steven do incredible work together, serving the needs of the Palestinian people with humanitarian aid programs and opportunities for Palestinians to interact with Israelis. David, the Orthodox Jew, has even helped Pastor Steven communicate the gospel to Palestinians!

How is this possible? Both Steven and David recognize the story they're in, and they joined the Author. They prioritized *the* story over *their* story. David, as a Jew, sees that he has an obligation to his neighbor and even more so to his Arab neighbors, who see themselves as the descendants of Ishmael. David, seeing his life as a part of *the* story feels an obligation to bring healing to the wound made by Abraham. Instead of rewriting the history of a patriarch, he acknowledges the fault and seeks a path of reconciliation. Steven, as a Christian, has the same obligation toward his neighbor and even more so his Jewish neighbors who provided the greatest path of reconciliation, Jesus. Steven, seeing his part of *the* story, welcomes the family reunion![38]

As we find ourselves in *the* story, we'll recognize the family reunion that's taking place. In the process we need to come to terms with the church's history of anti-Semitism. As the church, as a people, we will do well to cultivate a collective memory and see ourselves in the context of our history. In doing so, we can bring comfort and reconciliation; we can bind broken hearts. There are people who identify with Isaac and people who identify with Ishmael who have been wounded by those who identify with Jesus. We owe them a debt of repentance. Both have a redemptive purpose, and the church should empower them toward that end, toward their destiny.

9

"ABBA, WHAT'S A CHEESEBURGER?"

Occasionally I have the privilege of speaking at events with David Nekrutman during his visits to the United States. David often travels with his family and, on one occasion, he was traveling with his son, Ori. Ori was born in New York, and his family moved to Israel when he was a toddler. He has spent most of his life in Israel. After the event several of us went out for a bite to eat. Ori curiously inspected the menu, then leaned over to his father and asked, "Abba, what's a cheeseburger?" How does a ten-year-old-boy, born in the United States, not know about cheeseburgers!? Having grown up in a modern Orthodox home, spending the majority of his life in Israel, Ori obeyed the dietary restrictions compulsory for observant Jews—he kept kosher. One of those restrictions is the prohibition against mixing meat and dairy. Meat and cheese shall not meet; hence, his delayed discovery of the cheeseburger! Witnessing this interaction with Ori and his father, David, highlighted just how peculiar and fascinating the Jewish people are!

Ori, like all religious minorities, deserves to have a place of shelter and sanctuary where he can freely and proudly express his religious beliefs without fear of retribution. By virtue of the fact that they are, like all mankind, made in the image of God, the Jewish people deserve to have a home. And because of their matchless contribution to humanity, the nations of the world are indebted to that end. Spirituality aside, humanity has a moral obligation to the Jewish people.

The debate on college and university campuses regarding Israel is active, disproportionately anti-Israel, and too often fueled by sensationalism and fiction instead of reason and facts. The swelling wave of *criticism* against Israel is, at its core, one of the latest faces of an ancient and perpetual human epidemic: anti-Semitism. Accusations of apartheid have become *factual statements* due to their regularity and the widespread affirmation they receive from faculty. For a college student to publicly address the state of Israel as "the apartheid state of Israel" is commonplace and rarely challenged. The Boycott Sanction and Divestment (BDS) movement is another demonstration of animosity toward Israel and the Jewish people. Groups such as the Muslim Student Association and Students for Justice in Palestine (both finding their ideological origins in the radical Islamic ideology of the Muslim Brotherhood) work tirelessly to vilify Israel and anyone, Jew or Gentile, who supports her.[1]

One of the largest chapters of the Muslim Student Association is located at the University of California–Irvine. This organization attracted national attention during a visit from the Israeli ambassador to the United States, Michael Oren. The ambassador's speech was disrupted by Muslim students, ten of whom where later convicted by a jury for illegally disrupting the speech.

During a visit to the UC–Irvine campus, I saw two young men sitting outside of a coffee shop, with their Bibles open and having a time of prayer. I approached these young men, began some small talk, and proceeded to ask them what they thought about what was happening on their campus. Their very visible display of faith in a public place suggested they were serious about their faith, and I was curious to know how they viewed the hostile anti-Israel sentiment on their campus. The answer I received was disappointing but, sadly, not unexpected. To their credit, their response in no way discounted the authenticity of their faith, but the quality of the response was indicative of what has become an apathetic (and arguably irrelevant) Christian subculture in the Western world: "It's just sin. People need the gospel."

The challenge with that response is that it's not wrong! Essentially, sin is the problem and the gospel is the answer. This basic one-dimensional, albeit correct, response allows complacency and reveals a significant level of disconnect from the identity of Jesus and the responsibility of those who know him as Messiah, Lord, and Savior.

The young woman who was witness to my Peter-like "foot in the mouth" statement on the flight to Israel was conscious of her connection to her people. It influenced how she related to her present and looked to her future. For Christians, the fact that many are not consciously aware of, or familiar with, the progression of Christian thought, theology, and history doesn't mean we are free from their influences. As mentioned in chapter 6, the church began with a distinctly Hebraic mind-set, and that foundational way of thinking drastically changed within a few centuries. The response of the young men from UC–Irvine is an example of how we as Christians *think* today and how far removed it is from the Hebraic mind-set of the early church and an ethical concept of salvation.[2]

ON EARTH AS IT IS IN HEAVEN

Hebraic thought values the natural world and its relationship with the spiritual. The idea of "on earth as it is in heaven" wasn't introduced by Jesus; it was affirmed by Him. This Hebraic relationship between the natural and spiritual was displaced by a Greco-Roman dualistic view,[3] which contrasted the two and assigned value to each. The spiritual, eternal realm was deemed good and understood to constitute truth and reality. The natural realm was considered evil and temporary. One result of seeing the natural world as evil and temporary is that it renders history irrelevant against a permanent eternal reality, and the church becomes disconnected from the progression of redemptive history. This dualistic Greco-Roman view makes it difficult, if not impossible, to find ourselves in a biblical narrative that's moving toward a climax. Furthermore, our ethical view of salvation is seemingly lost. Our salvation focuses on escape instead of transformation.[4] We forsake our role as redemptive agents and our task to bring heaven to earth.

In keeping the main thing the main thing, let's revisit the topic of eternal life. The idea of salvation in the minds of many Christians has more to do with the afterlife than with this life. The language and approach of modern evangelism often focuses on *what happens when you die?* Will you go to heaven or hell? I'm not suggesting in any way that these questions aren't relevant to salvation, nor am I suggesting that the questions shouldn't be asked. I'm using them to identify how salvation is currently understood. I've often handed out pamphlets on the street and asked people the question, "If you die tonight, where would you go, heaven or hell?" In these scenarios, be it on a street corner or at a church altar, salvation is accessed through repeating someone else's words. And the initial presentation of salvation, in many cases, has little to do with *this* life. In no way am I trying to invalidate the genuine salvation experience people have on street corners or at church altars—I'm one of them! My point is that our presentation of, and invitation to, salvation can help us evaluate our present view of salvation itself. As Marvin Wilson stated in *Abraham Our Father,* this current idea would have made no sense to the early church:

> To the Hebrew mind a human being was a dynamic body-soul unity, called to serve God his Creator passionately, with his whole being, within the physical world. Certainly, the godly of the Old Testament could never have brought themselves to sing such patently foreign and heterodox words as the following, which may be heard in certain churches today: "This world is not my home, I'm just a-passin' through" or "Some glad morning when this life is o'er, I'll fly away," or "When all my labors and trials are o'er, and I am safe on the beautiful shore." To any Hebrew of Bible times this kind of language would be unrealistic and irresponsible, a cop-out—seeking to abandon the present, material world, while focusing on the joys of the "truly" spiritual world to come.[5]

This manner of thinking can be traced back to early church fathers such as Origen, whose Platonic influences "can hardly be overestimated."[6] Some of the same voices that sowed the earliest and most potent seeds of anti-Semitism also created the initial distance between Hebraic thought and the church. That distance made room for a wedge that not only separated the church from Hebraic thought, it put the church in opposition to the synagogue and cultivated animosity toward the Jews.

Eternal life, as Jesus defined it, was a present-tense reality, not a far-off, otherworldly experience! The way we think about salvation has sweeping consequences. The one-dimensional response from the young men at the coffee shop suggests that we are only saved *from something* (an eternity in hell) and fails to place appropriate emphasis on the fact that we are saved *to Someone* and that salvation carries with it a redemptive purpose and a redemptive responsibility.

Consider the Lord's Prayer:

> Our Father in heaven, hallowed be your name. Your kingdom come, your will be done, on earth as it is in heaven. Give us this day our daily bread, and forgive us our debts, as we also have forgiven our debtors. And lead us not into temptation, but deliver us from evil. (Matt. 6:9–13)

It is appropriate for us to first acknowledge the very first word, "Our." It's incredible how much is wrapped up in this one word! Jesus affirms a collective identity over an individual identity. Individualism, a concept celebrated in contemporary Christian thinking, finds little, if any, praise or substance in Scripture or the Hebraic mind-set. While individualism is not criticized, it is certainly not exalted the way we find it today. The knowledge of God is something that can only be apprehended in relationship with others.

One of the earliest movements in the church was monasticism, which "stressed seclusion from the world and society by withdrawal to a private life of faith."[7] This is not to say that monasticism was in error or of no value to the church.[8] However, it's important to identify that this way of thinking had, and continues to wield, significant influence on the church and is distinct from the emphasis on corporate identity in the Hebraic mind-set.

Jesus' reference to the kingdom and its connection to earth is where we will find our primary focus. Jesus, the Jewish people of his day, and the Jewish leaders who comprised the early church understood this connection and dynamic intersection between heaven and earth, temporal and eternal, spiritual and natural. To understand both Jesus and how to please Him, we need to recover this hermeneutic and allow it to deeply reshape the way we communicate and walk out our salvation. Inherent in the very nature of prayer is the concept of bringing heaven to earth . . . eternal life is NOW!

I am regularly astonished by the fascinating stories of people I meet in Israel. One such story comes from an artist who currently lives in the desert town of Arad. His story is nearly beyond belief. With no Jewish heritage or any religious identification with Christianity, he came to Israel in the '60s to work on a kibbutz (a communal settlement). He eventually became fluent in Hebrew, participated in the Israel Defense Force, and gained citizenship—all of which is almost entirely unheard of for non-Jews who come to Israel. Sculpting is his main craft, and his work can be appreciated as an act of intercession as much as it can be recognized as art. His work is done prayerfully in active fellowship with the Lord.

His series *Fountain of Tears* depicts the final utterances of Jesus in dialogue with a Holocaust survivor. He takes two of the most powerful elements of history for the Jewish people, Jesus and the Holocaust, and puts them together. What he produced in this process of *prophetic art* is emotionally captivating, proactive, and revelatory. After meeting the artist, I decided to bring a group of college students to the sculpture garden at his home in Israel.

One of the final pieces in the series is a re-creation of an oven door from a Nazi concentration camp. These ovens were used to cremate the remains of Jewish people after they were murdered. On the inside of the door is a child curled up in a fetal position. The imagery is intense yet not insensitive. It's forcefully delicate. The child's arm is reaching through the closed oven door, and the hand, as it reaches the other side of the door, is full of earth. Sitting next to me, listening to the artist explain this piece, was a young Native American believer. When the artist explained that the earth the child was holding was Israel, she became undone. She began to weep, and there was something precious, even holy, about it. I felt the Lord direct my attention to her in that moment because he had something he wanted to teach me.

As a Native American, like the Jewish student on my flight to Israel (see chapter 6), she knows what it means to be a part of a people. She shared a collective memory and identity with her tribe. What I witnessed in that moment of holy lament was someone who understood what it means to have your identity connected to the earth, to a homeland.

Perhaps the most consequential effect of having a view of salvation that is not fully integrated in the physical world is that we lose a disregard for the sacredness of space. As that young woman wept, I remembered someone else who lamented over a homeland, over a sacred place.

In Matthew 23:37 and Luke 13:34 we find Jesus lamenting over Jerusalem:

O Jerusalem, Jerusalem, the city that kills the prophets and stones those who are sent to it! How often would I have gathered your children together as a hen gathers her brood under her wings, and you were not willing!

The illustration that Jesus uses is of utmost importance and represents a singularity in Scripture. The word for "hen" is only used in Matthew and Luke as Jesus laments over the city of Jerusalem. In comparison to the rest of the Bible, the imagery of God when a bird is employed is typically a noble bird of flight. This reference to a hen is deliberately intimate and familial. It speaks of home and of family. Jesus was not prone to exaggeration, and this isolated word picture is profoundly connected to the emotions of Jesus, the history of the Jewish people, and Jesus' return. This moment carries the weight of the story and the family affair.

At this point we have noted several commonly known portions of scripture: Jeremiah 31 and the promise of the new covenant; Romans 12:1, with Paul's admonition to present ourselves as a "living sacrifice"; and Ephesians' glorious proclamation of God's saving grace, all of which are directly connected to Israel's place in God's story. This moment of Jesus' holy lament is no different. We can find the origin of His emotions in another widely used portion of scripture. It's stunning what you find when you just look at the next verse!

In 2 Chronicles 7 we find verses commonly used in prayer services and regularly associated with America's National Day of Prayer. Verse 14 reads, "If my people who are called by my name humble themselves, and pray and seek my face and turn from their wicked ways, then I will hear from heaven and will forgive their sin and heal their land." So, what's the next verse? "Now my eyes will be open and my ears attentive to the prayer that is made in this place." "This place" is Jerusalem! In the following verse we see the origin of Jesus' emotions: "For now I have chosen and consecrated this house that my name may be there forever. My *eyes* and my *heart* will be there for all time" (v. 17). Does "for all time" sound familiar? These are the same Hebrew words used in Jeremiah 31:36 when God says, "If this fixed order departs from before me, declares the LORD, then shall the offspring of Israel cease from being a nation before me forever."

These verses in 2 Chronicles give the account of the dedication of the temple in Jerusalem. Thirteen generations after God spoke these words to Solomon and the nation of Israel, His *heart* and His *eyes* stood on the Mount of Olives perfectly and miraculously incarnated in the person of Jesus! When God says "forever," He means it!

Some theologians argue that Jesus didn't make any direct territorial claims, and therefore the *land* was of no importance to Him, nor should it be to the church. It wasn't a direct claim because it was obvious to His audience and unmistakably present in the Old Testament. Removing the significance of the land apparently requires an agenda and a PhD! It's a matter of theological conjecture that runs contrary to the full counsel of Scripture, the character of God, and history's testimony of His faithfulness.

Theology that strips *the land* of value strips all land of value. The temporal, natural world is not understood as sacred, and we forsake the aspect of redemption, which will restore creation to what God created it to be: good. When the natural is not sacred or holy, land, like history, is irrelevant.[9]

The prevalence of this Greco-Roman paradigm is why Bethlehem and Nazareth have largely been forsaken by the Protestant world. Jerusalem (excluding the Temple Mount) is the only location in the biblical heartland where Christians are free to worship. That privilege is afforded us by Israel. However, Hebron, Bethlehem, Shiloh, Shechem, Bethel, and locations in Judea and Samaria (West Bank) of great consequence to the biblical narrative are subject to the religious intolerance of Islam.

Imagine if the same conversation I had at UC–Irvine took place in Berlin, Germany, in April 1933 after the Nazis organized a boycott of Jewish businesses. It's reasonable to believe that I would have received the same response, and history reveals the predominant apathy of the church leading up to and during the Holocaust.

There were, of course, exceptions: heroic Christians such as Corrie Ten Boom, Martin Niemoller, and Dietrich Bonhoeffer. Bonhoeffer is truly an extraordinary case, one whose life is the antithesis of the apathy yielded by a nearsighted view of the gospel and a shallow appreciation of being joined to God's redemptive purpose. Bonhoeffer was a German pastor who immediately opposed Hitler and the Nazi ideology. He was eventually arrested and executed for conspiring to kill Hitler. A man known for his stance as a Christian pacifist was so moved by the evil of his day that he was compelled to take action. Words which have been attributed to him serve as a sobering and haunting charge to us today: "Silence in the face of evil is itself evil: God will not hold us guiltless. Not to speak is to speak. Not to act is to act."[10]

There was another German who resisted the Nazis, this time much younger, and a woman. Her name was Sophie Scholl, and she was one of the leaders (along with her brother Hans) of the student group the White Rose at Munich University. Sophie was a devout Christian who, in 1942, as the war on the Russian front turned disastrous for Germany and as more and more reports filtered back about the slaughter of Jews and other innocents, decided to take a stand against the Nazi state and Adolf Hitler. The White Rose authored six pamphlets and printed thousands of them and then distributed them to ordinary German citizens by looking up their addresses in phone books. One can't help but be amazed that the words of these pamphlets were written by university students. Sophie herself was only twenty-one at the time. Here is one brief sample of what these brave students wrote in their fourth pamphlet:

> Every word that comes from Hitler's mouth is a lie. When he says peace, he means war, and when he blasphemously uses the name of the Almighty, he means the power of evil, the fallen angel, Satan. His mouth is the foul-smelling maw of Hell, and his might is at bottom accursed. True, we must conduct a struggle against the National Socialist terrorist state with rational means; but whoever today still doubts the reality, the existence of demonic powers, has failed by a wide margin to understand the metaphysical background of this war. Behind the concrete, the visible events, behind all objective, logical considerations, we find the irrational element: The struggle against the demon, against the servants of the Antichrist. Everywhere and at all times demons have been lurking in the dark, waiting for the moment when man is weak; when of his own volition he leaves his place in the order of Creation as founded for him by God in freedom;

when he yields to the force of evil, separates himself from the powers of a higher order; and after voluntarily taking the first step, he is driven on to the next and the next at a furiously accelerating rate. Everywhere and at all times of greatest trial men have appeared, prophets and saints who cherished their freedom, who preached the One God and who His help brought the people to a reversal of their downward course. Man is free, to be sure, but without the true God he is defenseless against the principle of evil. He is a like rudderless ship, at the mercy of the storm, an infant without his mother, a cloud dissolving into thin air.

I ask you, you as a Christian wrestling for the preservation of your greatest treasure, whether you hesitate, whether you incline toward intrigue, calculation, or procrastination in the hope that someone else will raise his arm in your defense? Has God not given you the strength, the will to fight? We must attack evil where it is strongest, and it is strongest in the power of Hitler.[11]

Shortly after the disastrous German defeat at the Battle of Stalingrad, Sophie and the rest of the leaders of the White Rose were caught, rounded up, subjected to interrogation by the Gestapo, and brought before a show trial of the "People's Court" meant to intimidate the population against any hint of resistance. Joseph Goebbels, the Reich minister for propaganda, had just given a speech calling for "total war," which was meant to rouse the German people to victory after the catastrophes on the eastern front. The Nazis were out for blood.

But what makes Sophie's story so compelling is that she was given a choice: because she was a woman, she was given a chance to recant what she had said against the Führer and thereby avoid death. But this young woman, barely out of her teen years and with her whole life ahead of her, said *"No!"* She knew she was right, and the Nazis were wrong; and even though she could have saved her life, she stood up for the truth. She did this not because she was vain or arrogant or stubborn, but because she knew that what was at stake was a cosmic struggle bigger than herself and that the sort of devil's bargain she was offered had already been accepted by far too many Germans and had already led to the slaughter of millions. Sophie was quickly guillotined by the so-called People's Court.

For Christians today to remain apathetic and disengaged from the evils of our day, and specifically from issues surrounding Israel and the Jewish people, I believe, would be an example of what Bonhoeffer described as "cheap grace."[12] Our story isn't what we make it to be. Rather, our story is discovered when we find God in *the* story and join Him. Anything else is too great and too marvelous. Like King David, when we calm and quiet our souls, when we embrace God's sovereign design of our story, we will fulfill the purpose of God in our generation. Like Sophie Scholl, we can do the dangerous and difficult work of exposing the "irrational elements" behind the "visible events" and embrace a faith that surpasses "logical considerations" and arrives at the impossible, even if it means a literal or proverbial death before a so-called People's Court.

10

THE ROAD TO OZ

If I had to choose one portion of scripture that embodies my motivation in writing this book, it would be Joshua 5:13–15. In this passage, Joshua, like Abraham and Moses before him, encounters the Lord. After forty years of wandering, Joshua and the Hebrew nation he is charged to lead celebrate the first Passover in the Promised Land, outside Jericho. Joshua sees a man approaching with sword drawn and asks, "Are you for us, or for our adversaries?" The response Joshua receives is what reverberates in my heart as I write this book: "No, but I am the commander of the army of the LORD. Now I have come."

The commander of the Lord's army ignores the options presented by Joshua; he introduces himself and states the obvious, "Now I have come." Joshua falls on his face in worship. Unlike angelic encounters we find in scripture, this commander receives Joshua's worship. Reminiscent of Moses and his encounter with the Lord at the burning bush, the commander instructs Joshua, "Take your sandals from your feet, for the place where you are standing is holy."

I believe the Lord has the same answer to that question today. If asked if He's taking sides, I think He would still say, "No."

We find God's echoes of the Lord's "No" to Joshua in Ezekiel 36:22 when he says, "It is not for your sake, O house of Israel, that I am about to act, but for the sake of my holy name." We see it again in Jesus' High Priestly prayer in John 17:1, "Father, the hour has come; glorify your Son that the Son may glorify you," and again in Ephesians 2:8–9, "For by grace you have been saved through faith. And this is not your own doing; it is the gift of God, not a result of works, so that no one may boast." From Jericho to Ephesus, we see consistency in God's character, His moral perfection, and His justified self-glorification.

In that moment, outside the city of Jericho, what was obvious to Joshua is not always so obvious to us: knowing when the Lord has come.

David Nekrutman, my modern Orthodox Jewish friend, often speaks to Christian groups visiting Israel. On one occasion he said something I will never forget: "Not only are you watchmen [referencing Isaiah 62:6] to your community, but I am a watchman to my community because the cross is no longer scary to me!"

His statement represents a shift in Jewish thinking nearly eighteen hundred years in the making. To the average Jewish person—sharing a collective identify and memory—the name "Jesus" is synonymous with ghettoization and forced conversion at its best, and mass murder at its worst. From anti-Semitic writings of second-century church fathers, to the Crusades, to inquisitions, pogroms, and the Holocaust, all of them were done by the hands of "Christians." In our lifetime, this is shifting! It is miraculous, and it demands our attention. It's the Lord saying, "Now I have come."

Joshua's perspective was different from the Israelites of Jesus' day, and both are different from ours. Joshua was there at the beginning of the nation of Israel. Encounter and experience with God was the norm, not tradition and ritual.

If we're to recognize the Lord when He shows up, it would help to know where we are in the first place—especially in the Western world and particularly in America. We need to see our piece of the puzzle in the big picture and understand our moment in the story.

Biblical illiteracy is at an all-time high, secularization is on the rise,[1] and Western spirituality is drifting toward a "moralistic, therapeutic deism."[2] God, in the mind of the next generation, is more like a genie in a lamp than the awesome and majestic God of Abraham, Isaac, and Jacob. The God of moral, therapeutic deism is there to make *our* dreams come true. He's there to help us when we think we need it and bail us out when we suffer the consequences of our own actions. The following statements are in line with moralistic, therapeutic deism:

> "God wants people to be good, nice, and fair to each other, as taught in the Bible and most world religions."

> "The central goal of life is to be happy and to feel good about oneself."

> "God does not need to be particularly involved in one's life except when God is needed to resolve a problem."

> "Good people go to heaven when they die."[3]

Concepts of justification and sanctification are often diluted in, if not entirely absent from, mainline and even evangelical preaching. Therefore, they are not present in the working theology of most conservative Christian young people.[4] Life is about good choices and being happy. George Barna in his book, *The Second Coming of the Church*, has this to say about where we are as a *Christian* culture:

> We desire experience more than knowledge. We prefer choices to absolutes. We embrace preferences rather than truths. We seek comfort rather than growth. Faith must come on our terms or we reject it. We have enthroned ourselves as the final arbiters of righteousness, the ultimate rulers of our own experience and destiny. We are the Pharisees of the new millennium.[5]

I'm not the only person calling us Pharisees, even if we look a bit different than the Pharisees of Jesus' day. I think I was a little kinder, but if the shoe fits . . . let's start walking down the road.

Regardless of biblical literacy or basic understanding of the gospel, we know that we don't like bullies and we love the underdog! We love justice. We want to see the little guy win: the poor, the orphan, and the widow. And so does, God, right? God may have said, "No" to Joshua, but isn't God always on the side of the widow, the orphan, the poor, and the oppressed? God takes their side because He is always for the underdog, right? Yes and no.

The problem isn't God's allegiance to the widow, the orphan, and the poor. God is a God of deliverance, a God of justice. The problem is that He doesn't share our ideas of justice.

God is the ultimate and final authority of morality. What He says is justice is justice. Biblical justice is the actualization of redemptive purpose. Justice, God's justice, is all of creation fulfilling its God-given destiny and purpose.

JUST, NOT FAIR

As we examine our understanding of justice, like the Nazarenes in the synagogue with Jesus, we'll have a choice to make. Will we reject faith that doesn't "come on our terms" and "embrace preferences rather than truths?"

Our misunderstanding of justice is twofold. First, if we don't understand the basic doctrines of justification and sanctification, our approach to justice defaults to self-serving and narcissistic pity.

Consider the previously mentioned beliefs of moral, therapeutic deism: doing good gets me to heaven, and God wants me to feel good about myself. Both conclusions are contrary to the basic Christian doctrines of justification and sanctification. Sanctification, the process of being transformed into the image of Jesus, runs counter to the humanist idea that people are essentially good. When people are essentially good (not in need of transformation), justice is based on their inherent goodness, and they deserve to be happy.

Justification, our righteous standing before God because of the atoning work of Jesus, also confronts this humanist view. Our salvation is not merited by our actions and has little, if anything, to do with the idea that "good people go to heaven when they die." Our salvation is afforded us by Jesus.

When we fail to recognize justification and sanctification, we fail to engage in biblical justice. Doing justice is a means to personal salvation (doing good and going to heaven) instead of a response to the salvation provided through faith in Jesus. Additionally, our efforts at justice, when void of the basic doctrine of sanctification, do not embody the need for transformation. Instead of engaging in justice as a co-laborer with God (who saved me and wants to transform me and the world I'm in), it simply becomes whatever is the "nice" thing to do at any particular moment.

As Tim Keller stated in his book *Generous Justice*, "traditional doctrine rightly understood will lead to doing justice."[6] But without understanding basic doctrine, our view of justice is focused on equality, fairness, and humanist ideals espousing the lie that people are all essentially good. Justice, therefore, is most often understood as equality and fairness; in other words, everyone gets the same thing regardless of circumstance or redemptive purpose. A flawed view of justice can often conflict with biblical justice and the actualization of redemptive purpose. For example, consider Matthew 16:21–23:

> From that time Jesus began to show his disciples that he must go to Jerusalem and suffer many things from the elders and chief priests and scribes, and be killed, and on the third day be raised. And Peter took him aside and began to rebuke him, saying, "Far be it from you, Lord! This shall never happen to you." But he turned and said to Peter, "Get behind me, Satan! You are a hindrance to me. *For you are not setting your mind on the things of God, but on the things of man.*" (emphasis added)

The second problem is assigning moral value to the poor, the widow, and the orphan—the oppressed—regardless of their actions.[7] Michael Prell identifies this phenomenon in his deeply insightful book on the subject, *Underdogma*. He defines *underdogma* as "the belief that those who have less power are virtuous and noble—*because they have less power*—and the belief that those who have more power are to be scorned—*because they have more power.*"[8]

Underdogma is the reason why many are suspicious of megachurches and highly successful or wealthy people, and why American exceptionalism is such a controversial topic. Underdogma undergirds the "Palestinian liberation theology" of Naim Ateek and his position that God is on the side of the Palestinian because the Palestinian is oppressed and that God is always for the oppressed, regardless of their actions. In many cases this line of thinking makes room for the justification of deplorable acts such as suicide bombing.

Underdogma is what's made it possible for the world to identify Palestinian refugees as the world's underdog. It's also the reason Israel's enemies accuse Israel of being a colonialist, *imperialist contagion* in the Middle East, which, according to underdogma, you can't be much worse. However, both accusations are nothing more than propaganda fueled by cosmic powers in the heavens as the world "follows the prince of the power of the air."

Sadly, the world isn't the only one entertaining this argument: undiscerning Christians—the moralistic, therapeutic deists—are taking it hook, line, and sinker.

When I google "colonialism," I get the following definition: "the policy or practice of acquiring full or partial political control over another country, occupying it with settlers, and exploiting it economically." First of all, Judea, the uncontestable ancient name for the region home to the city of Jerusalem, is where we get the name "Jew"! Israel is the ancestral homeland of the Jewish people, and any contrary argument is likely motivated by a political or religious agenda—in most cases both. The region of Judea existed long before anyone ever called the region Palestine and long before anyone ever called himself a "Palestinian." The region was given the name Palestine in the second century by the Romans as an insult to the Jewish people. The name etymologically comes from the name of Israel's arch-enemy, the Philistines. Before the formation of the state of Israel, both Jews and Arabs were called "Palestinians." It was a regional name with no ethnic or national significance.

Second, the Jewish people have a legal right to live in their ancestral homeland, as noted in chapter 5. Third, the region known as Palestine was a wasteland at the turn of the nine-teenth century. No "colonialist" in his right mind would think to exploit the land because there was nothing to exploit. With desert to the south and malaria swamps to the north, the land was rendered undesirable for profitable exploitation. During a visit to the region in 1867, Mark Twain called it "a hopeless, dreary, heart-broken land" that "sits in sack cloth and ashes."[9]

Finally, the accusation of imperialism strains the imagina-tion for the historically literate. To call Jews imperialists would be laughable if the accusation weren't alive and well. Outside of malicious intent, one must be detached from any sense of his-tory, demography, or sociology to arrive at the conclusion that Jews are imperialists. The Hebrew Bible, as described by Rabbi Jonathan Sacks, is a "sustained protest against empire, hierarchy, ruling elites and the enslavement of the masses. Every individual is sacrosanct. Every life is sacred. The human person as such has inalienable dignity."[10] Jewish history itself is nothing but a series of tragedies in which the Jews fell victim to their far more powerful adversaries. Until 1948, they never had a country of their own; they were always a nation within a nation, and rarely, if ever, fully welcomed wherever they went.

Jews immigrating back to their ancestral homeland were in many ways similar to the major biblical journeys of the Bible: Abraham, Moses, and the Babylonian exiles. None of them was leaving a poor country for a rich country or a weak nation for a strong.[11] Contrary to an agenda of exploitation, Jewish immigration, as detailed in chapter 2, increased the quality of life for the preexisting population. Like Abraham, Moses, and the exiles, their motivation was eternal, not economic. They were compelled to *aliyah* by an irrevocable identification with the land. Only sovereign purpose has the magnetism capable of drawing *people* to desert, rocky hills, and malarial swamps. The people's return to the land was a transformation. It was a labor of redemption that actualized the potential of the land. The Jews were doing justice.

In a sadistic way it's almost a compliment to call the Jews imperialists. To believe that a people who are a fraction of a percent of the world's population are imperialists and planning to take over the world is to believe that the Jewish people are the most capable people to ever walk the earth. And there's the catch: they are! Leo Tolstoy said of the Jewish people:

> What kind of unique creature is this whom all the rulers of all the nations of the world have disgraced and crushed and expelled and destroyed; persecuted, burned and drowned, and who, despite their anger and their fury, continues to live and to

flourish. What is this Jew whom they have never succeeded in enticing with all the enticements in the world, whose oppressors and persecutors only suggested that he deny (and disown) his religion and cast aside the faithfulness of his ancestors?! The Jew—is the symbol of eternity. . . . He is the one who for so long had guarded the prophetic message and transmitted it to all mankind. A people such as this can never disappear. The Jew is eternal. He is the embodiment of eternity.[12]

The heart and the substance of the matter, Israel's place in *the story*, is this: the Jew is not a testimony of his own merit as much as he is a testimony of God's. One is forced to acknowledge the Jews' "embodiment of eternity." We can find courage in hardship and hope for the future as we observe the plight and prestige of promise, or we can rage against it, and ultimately contend with a sovereign and faithful God. We can be offended at God's sovereign purpose, or we can calm and quiet our souls.

Through Israel, the land and the people, we are seeing the covenant promises of God at work, right before our eyes. We are seeing on full display the power of the God who uses the foolish things to shame the wise, the weak things to shame the strong, the low and despised to shame the high and the exalted, and the things which are not to shame the things that are (1 Cor. 1:27–28). I believe one of the biggest reasons the world cannot bear the continued existence of the Jewish people, let alone their resurrection in the land of Israel as a self-governing nation, is that they provide the most contemporary, clear, undeniable, and blatant sign that the God of the Bible is alive, active, and faithful to the words and promises He penned through Moses, the prophets, Jesus, and the apostles. It has little to do with

Israel, and everything to do with God. In our own day, the existence of Israel in the land of Israel is the biggest jab in the eye to those who say God does not exist and that the God of the Bible is a Bronze Age myth.

Israel is God's "I told you" to the world, the great sign in our own time that He is there, that He is not silent, and that the agendas of men—no matter how well planned, executed, and conceived—will not stand against the sovereign will of the Lord of history, the God of covenant, the God of Abraham, Isaac, and Jacob. God still has His hands in the dirt, and Israel echoes to the nations the same question Jesus asked His disciples, "Who do you say I am?"

If God can keep His promise to Israel, if He can secure the passage and preservation of this feisty Hebrew tribe through human history, surely He is trustworthy and more than able to keep His promise to us. If the land and the people of promise are still here and reunited against all odds, I can hope, against all odds, that God will continue to fulfill His word. I can find courage in God's promise of full redemption and final justice.

Not only is my expectation of the future hopeful; I also find Scripture to be a reliable guide as I search for where my piece of the puzzle fits in the big picture. The Bible fuels my efforts, my active decisions to calm and quiet my soul and embrace sovereignty. The preservation of the Jewish people and the State of Israel is God's invitation to the nations of the earth. In many ways it's the answer to the psalmist's prayer in Psalm 83:18, "that they may know that you alone, whose name is the LORD, are the Most High over all the earth." The main thing is the main thing. God is not about Israel, and Israel is not about Israel: Israel is about God, and God is about Himself.

Psalm 83 brings another heart issue to the table, which warrants our attention. The enemies of Israel from millennia past and the enemies of today have the same goal in mind: a world without Israel, without Jews. The earliest archaeological reference to Jerusalem is a curse written on an Egyptian execration text (20th–19th century BCE), basically an ancient voodoo doll.[13] From time immemorial, empire after empire, ideology after ideology, have attempted to take the land and the people of God's promise and erase them from the earth. Despite all their efforts, generation after generation, they have all failed.

Psalm 83 clearly and prophetically depicts Israel's enemies,[14] their plot of destruction, and the Lord's victory over them.[15] In a cultural climate that fosters moralistic, therapeutic deism, when traditional values are questioned and moral relativism continues to metastasize, most of us don't want to do the hard work[16] of reconciling a God who can fulfill promises and display faithfulness in and through war.

A dear friend (who describes herself as "Israeli by choice" after making aliyah from Canada the moment she was old enough to do so) introduced me to the profundity of the Hebrew word *oz*. In Psalm 29:11, we find a prayer that gets to the core of the matter: "May the LORD give strength to his people! May the LORD bless his people with peace!" The word *oz* is often translated as "strength," but it means so much more. *Oz* is courage, valor, and heroism. It's a grand, virtuous strength. What's most important, and what my friend showed me, is that *oz* comes before another Hebrew word found in this prayer: *shalom*. *Shalom*, a word more familiar to non-Hebrew speakers, means "peace." However, *shalom*, like *oz*, has a deeper, fuller meaning. It's not just peace; it is prosperity and wholeness.

In a way it's like being "a weaned child with its mother" and experiencing not only the absence of conflict but the fullness of purpose. God places *oz* before *shalom*, and I believe God (our benevolent loving Father, who is morally perfect) did so with good reason. Without virtuous strength there will be no prosperity, no wholeness, no justice.

It's time to put our shoes on and start walking down the road, to continue thinking honestly and courageously, and to do some difficult work. I trust that our road to *oz* will lead to an encounter with the Lord and set us on a path of confident hope. Early on we looked at the continuity of the family affair in scripture. We saw the cover-to-cover representation of a Jewish Jesus, from Matthew to Revelation. In Joshua 5, in the commander of the Lord's army, we find a representation of Jesus that finds its symmetry in the book of Revelation:

> Then I saw heaven opened, and behold, a white horse! The one sitting on it is called Faithful and True, and *in righteousness he judges and makes war* . . . He is clothed in a robe dipped in blood, and the name by which he is called is The Word of God. And the armies of heaven arrayed in fine linen, white and pure, were following him on white horses. From his mouth comes a sharp sword with which to *strike down the nations*, and he will rule them with a rod of iron. He will tread the winepress of the fury of the wrath of God the Almighty. (Rev. 19:11, 13–15, emphasis added)

If we want to see real justice, we need to understand its Author—the only Faithful and True judge. Biblical justice is not about "everyone getting the same thing"[17] or personal happiness. The kingdom of God is just, not fair; and biblical justice is the actualization of redemptive purpose, not necessarily the equal distribution of temporal benefits. Biblical justice is avoiding what is "too great" and "too marvelous" (see chapter 7), embracing your heavenly Father's sovereign wisdom and kindness, so that you can calm and quiet your soul. Biblical justice is realized when people are empowered to find themselves in *the story*.

The information age, with all its First World luxuries, has provided a quality of life that far surpasses that of previous generations. A worldview influenced by First World comforts, the Enlightenment, moral relativism, and multiculturalism cannot "grasp that conflict and war have been the norm, and peace has been the exception in human experience."[18]

Shalom follows *oz*; but peace accomplished through human strength, while valuable and honorable, is always temporary. The next great sea change in *the story* will involve nations being struck down, judgment, and war. However, this judgment and this display of power will be heavenly, and the end result will be divine, eternal shalom. Nonetheless, one does not come without the other. When we fail to recognize this, we fail to comprehend biblical peace and justice; we fail to recognize "the God of earth and history, the Creator of this world, in the here and now."[19] We miss the Son of God mysteriously and inexorably found in the son of Joseph.

The Hebrew language, in its modern and biblical forms, has more to teach us. In this our insight will derive from the depth of a word and a word that's missing. The modern Hebrew word for *history* is *historia*. It's a transliteration of the English word *history*. Hebrew doesn't have a word for "history" as there is no biblical Hebrew root word that serves to generate the word. Instead of *history*, the biblical Hebrew offers the word *remember*. The Hebrew word *zâkar* means "remember." And, as you've most likely guessed, it has a wealth of meaning like other Hebrew words. While *history* is academic and passive, *remember* is active and emotional. When God *remembers* in the Bible, it's not a basic recollection of information, events, or people; it's *acting* on behalf of information, events, and people. When God *remembered* Noah in Genesis 8:1, He did so by acting, by "coming to his rescue."[20] When He *remembered* His covenant with Abraham, Isaac, and Jacob (Ex. 2:24) He delivered the Hebrews from Egyptian bondage. When He *remembered* His covenant with David, He blessed future kings of Israel, and ultimately sent Jesus from David's line.

While sitting next to that young, Jewish college student on my flight to Israel (see chapter 6), I failed to appreciate the *history* of the Jewish people. But she didn't fail to *remember*. As the church, we need to not just study the history of the Jews, but *remember* it.

In Exodus 1:8, the Bible tells us, "There arose a new king over Egypt, who did not know Joseph." The king and the people forgot. They forgot about this Hebrew slave who had miraculously ascended from sitting in a dungeon on trumped-up charges to ruling the empire as Pharaoh's second in command. With divine wisdom, Joseph prepared for a devastating famine, sparing the Egyptians from want and suffering. In the process he also saved his family, the descendants of Abraham, Isaac, and Jacob.

The Egyptians didn't appreciate the history of the Hebrews in their midst. Jealousy turned to fear, and fear turned to the Hebrews' enslavement. But God *remembered*. He remembered His promise; He remembered His covenant. As partakers of that same covenant, through the blood of Jesus (Eph. 2:13), we need to *remember*. The existence of the modern State of Israel and the preservation of the Jewish people call us to remember. The apostle Paul calls us, in light of God's saving grace, to *remember* the covenants of promise (Eph. 2:11). Jesus, instituting the new covenant, raised a cup symbolic of God's deliverance, and issued an eternal charge to His first disciples and to all who would come after: *remember*! (Luke 22:19; 1 Cor. 11:25).

The church has fully embraced the blessings of covenant. We also need to fully embrace the *responsibility* of covenant. Returning to the church's roots, we need to restore the ethical scope of salvation. Eternal life beckons us to be agents of redemption and to do justice. In order to do so we must acknowledge and submit to the Author of justice. While comparisons to the Arab-Israeli conflict have been made to demonstrate the illogical double standards to which Israel is held, the Arab-Israeli conflict is not just another conflict. Israel is not just another nation. The Jews and the Palestinians are not just another example, in the long history of examples, of people groups in conflict. Jerusalem is not just another city. By God's design, the future of that nation and those people affect the future of all people and all nations.

I don't pretend to offer "solutions" to the Arab-Israeli conflict but rather to place it in the larger context of redemptive history and illuminate that God has placed upon us a co-responsibility for the course of history.[21]

For Dietrich Bonhoeffer and Sophie Scholl, it meant sacrificing personal perspective and preservation. But, they did so because they were compelled by an eternal sense of responsibility. Inevitably, our role as active participant will conflict with cultural norms and, at times (similar to when Peter confronted

Jesus), it will be contrary to our most logical and sincere convictions. It should be no surprise to us that to find our life we must lose it and to be Jesus' disciple we must pick up our cross and follow Him.

Psalm 25:14 says, "The friendship of the LORD is for those who fear him, and he makes known to them his covenant." My prayer for you is that the knowledge of God will empower you to be an agent of justice and redemption, and that He would make His covenant known to you and lead you to *your* place in *His* story.

APPENDIX I

CHRISTIAN ANTI-SEMITISM

(Courtesy of ReligiousTolerance.org.)

ANTI-JUDAISM: 70 TO 1200 CE
PERSECUTION OF JEWS BY ROMAN PAGANS:

70 The Roman Army destroyed Jerusalem, killed over 1 million Jews, took about 100,000 into slavery and captivity, and scattered many from Palestine to other locations in the Roman Empire.

132 "Bar Kochba led a hopeless three-year revolt against the Roman Empire. Many Jews had accepted him as the Messiah. About a half-million Jews were killed; thousands were sold into slavery or taken into captivity. The rest were exiled from Palestine and scattered throughout the known world, adding to what is now called the '*Diaspora*.' Judaism was no longer recognized as a legal religion.[1]

306 The Church *Synod of Elvira* banned marriages, sexual intercourse and community contacts between Christians and Jews.[2,3]

325 The *Council of Nicea* decided to separate the celebration of Easter from the Jewish Passover. They stated: *"For it is unbecoming beyond measure that on this holiest of festivals we should follow the customs of the Jews. Henceforth let us have nothing in common with this odious people . . . We ought not, therefore, to have anything in common with the Jews . . . our worship follows a . . . more convenient course . . . we desire dearest brethren, to separate ourselves from the detestable company of the Jews . . . How, then, could we follow these Jews, who are almost certainly blinded."*

339 Converting to Judaism became a criminal offense.

380 The Bishop of Milan was responsible for the burning of a synagogue; he referred to it as *"an act pleasing to God."*

528 Emperor Justinian (527–564) passed the Justinian Code. It prohibited Jews from building synagogues, reading the Bible in Hebrew, assembling in public, celebrating Passover before Easter, and testifying against Christians in court.[4]

613 Very serious persecution began in Spain. Jews were given the options of either leaving Spain or converting to Christianity. Jewish children over six years of age were taken from their parents and given a Christian education.

694 The 17th Church *Council of Toledo*, Spain defined Jews as the serfs of the prince. This was based, in part, on the beliefs

by Chrysostom, Origen, Jerome, and other church Fathers that God punished the Jews with perpetual slavery because of their responsibility for the execution of Jesus.[5]

722 Leo III outlawed Judaism. Jews were baptized against their will.

855 Jews were exiled from Italy.

1078 "Pope Gregory VII decreed that Jews could not hold office or be superiors to Christians."[6]

1096 The *First Crusade* launched. Although the prime goal of the crusades was to liberate Jerusalem from the Muslims, Jews were a second target. As the soldiers passed through Europe on the way to the Holy Land, large numbers of Jews were challenged: "*Christ-killers, embrace the Cross or die!*" [Twelve thousand] Jews in the Rhine Valley alone were killed in the first Crusade. This behavior continued for [eight] additional crusades, until the [ninth] in 1272.

1099 The Crusaders forced all of the Jews of Jerusalem into a central synagogue and set it on fire. Those who tried to escape were forced back into the burning building.

1146 The Second Crusade began. A French Monk, Rudolf, called for the destruction of the Jews.

1180 The French King of France, Philip Augustus, arbitrarily seized all Jewish property and expelled the Jews from the country. There was no legal justification for this action. They were allowed to sell all movable possessions, but their land and houses were stolen by the king.

1189 Jews were persecuted in England. The Crown claimed all Jewish possessions. Most of their houses were burned.

ANTI-JUDAISM: *1201 TO 1800 CE*
PERSECUTION OF JEWS BY CHRISTIANS CONTINUES.

1205 Pope Innocent III wrote to the archbishops of Sens and Paris that "*the Jews, by their own guilt, are consigned to perpetual servitude because they crucified the Lord . . . As slaves rejected by God, in whose death they wickedly conspire, they shall by the effect of this very action, recognize themselves as the slaves of those whom Christ's death set free . . .*

1229 The Spanish inquisition starts. Later, in 1252, Pope Innocent IV authorizes the use of torture by the Inquisitors.

1306 100,000 Jews are exiled from France. They left with only the clothes on their backs, and food for only one day.

1321 In Guienne [or, Guyenne], France, Jews were accused of having incited criminals to poison wells. 5,000 Jews were burned alive, at the stake.

1347+ Ships from the Far East carried rats into Mediterranean ports. The rats carried the Black Death. At first, fleas spread the disease from the rats to humans. As the plague worsened, the germs spread from human to human. In five years, the death toll had reached 25 million. In England centuries passed before its population levels recovered from the plague. People searched for someone to blame. *They noted that a smaller percentage of Jews than Christians caught the disease. This was undoubtedly due to the Jewish sanitary and dietary laws, which had been preserved from Old Testament times.* Rumors circulated that Satan was protecting the Jews and that they were paying back the Devil by poisoning wells used by Christians. The solution was to torture, murder and burn the Jews. *"In Bavaria . . . 12,000 Jews . . . perished; in the small town of Erfurt . . . 3,000; Rue Brulée . . . 2,000 Jews; near Tours, an immense trench was dug, filled with blazing wood and in a single day 160 Jews were burned."*[7] In Strausberg 2,000 Jews were burned. In Maintz 6,000 were killed . . . ; in Worms 400 . . ."[8]

1354 12,000 Jews were executed in Toledo.

1434 *"Jewish men in Augsburg had to sew yellow buttons to their clothes. Across Europe, Jews were forced to wear a long undergarment, an overcoat with a yellow patch, bells and tall pointed yellow hats with a large button on them."*[9]

1453 The Franciscan monk, Capistrano, persuaded the King of Poland to terminate all Jewish civil rights.

1492 Jews were given the choice of being baptized as Christians or being banished from Spain. 300,000 left Spain penniless. Many migrated to Turkey, where they found tolerance among the Muslims. Others converted to Christianity but often continued to practice Judaism in secret.

1516 The Governor of the Republic of Venice decided that Jews would be permitted to live only in one area of the city. It was located in the South Girolamo parish and was called the *"Ghetto Novo." This was the first ghetto in Europe. Hitler made use of the concept in the 1930's.*

1523 Martin Luther distributed his essay *"That Jesus Was Born a Jew."* He hoped that large numbers of Jews would convert to Christianity. They didn't, and he began to write and preach hatred against them. Luther has been condemned in recent years for being extremely antisemitic. The charge has some merit; however he was probably typical of most Christians during his era.

1555 **July 12:** A Roman Catholic Papal bull, *"Cum nimis absurdum,"* required Jews to wear badges and live in ghettos. They were not allowed to own property outside the ghetto. Living conditions were dreadful: over 3,000 people were forced to live in about eight acres of land. Women had to wear a yellow veil or scarf; men had to wear a piece of yellow cloth on their hat.[10]

ANTI-SEMITISM: RACIALLY-BASED PERSECUTION OF JEWS
1800 to 1945, Including the Holocaust, or the Shoah Persecution of Jews by Christians continues. The conversion from religiously-based to racially-based persecution:

PRIOR TO 1800 *CE* Persecution was directed at followers of Judaism because of their religious belief; it has been referred to as anti-Judaism. CE, Jews could escape oppression by converting to Christianity, and being baptized. The Christian church taught in past centuries that *all* Jews (past, present and future) were responsible for Jesus' death. The church also believed that some Jews must be allowed to live, because the biblical book of Revelation indicated that they had a role to play in the "end times." They concluded that it was acceptable to make Jews' lives quite miserable.

SINCE ABOUT 1800 CE " . . . Nationalism became a dominant value in the Western and Arab worlds . . . anti-Semitism increasingly focused on the Jews' peoplehood and nationhood." Persecution became a form of racism, and has generally been called "anti-Semitism"—a word "created by an anti-Semite, Wilhelm Marr [in 1879]. Marr's intention was to replace the German word Judenhass (Jew-hatred) with a term that would make Jew-haters sound less vulgar and even somewhat scientific." The word anti-Semite is not a particularly good choice, because the root word "Semitic" refers to a group of languages, not to a single language or to a race, people or nation. However, it is in near-universal usage.

ANTI-SEMITISM: PERSECUTION OF JEWS ALONG RACIAL LINES:
Subsequent attacks against Jews tended to be racially motivated. They were perpetrated primarily by the state. The Jewish people were viewed as a separate people or race.

¹"JEWRY'S VICTORY OVER TEUTONISM."

1881 Alexander II of Russia was assassinated by radicals. The Jews were blamed. About 200 individual pogroms against the Jews followed. ("*Pogrom*" is a Russian word meaning "*devastation*" or "*riot*." In Russia, a pogrom was typically a mob riot against

Jewish individuals, shops, homes or businesses. They were often supported and even organized by the government.) Thousands of Jews became homeless and impoverished. The few who were charged with offenses generally received very light sentences.[11]

1894 **Captain Alfred Dreyfus, an officer on the French general staff, was convicted of treason**. The evidence against him consisted of a piece of paper from his wastebasket with another person's handwriting, and papers forged by antisemitic officers. He received a life sentence on Devil's Island, off the coast of South America. The French government was aware that a Major Esterhazy was actually guilty.[12] The church, government and army united to suppress the truth. Writer Emile Zola and politician Jean Jaurès fought for justice and human rights. After 10 years, the French government fell and Drefus was declared totally innocent. **The Dreyfus Affair was worldwide news for years. It motivated Journalist Theodor Herzl to write a book in 1896: "*The Jewish State: A Modern Solution to the Jewish Question.*" The book led to the founding of the Zionist movement which fought for a Jewish Homeland. A half century later, the state of Israel was born.**

1905 **The Okhrana, the Russian secret police in the reign of Czar Nicholas II, converted an earlier anti-Semitic novel into a document called the "*Protocols of the Elders of Zion.*"** It was published privately in 1897. A Russian Orthodox priest, Sergius Nilus, published them publicly in 1905. It was promoted as the record of "*secret rabbinical conferences whose aim was to subjugate and exterminate the Christians.*"[13] The Protocols were used by the Okhrana in a propaganda campaign that was associated with massacres of the Jews. These were the Czarist Pogroms of 1905.

1915 600,000 Jews were forcibly moved from the western borders of Russia towards the interior. About 100,000 died of exposure or starvation.

1917 *"In the civil war following the Bolshevik Revolution of 1917, the reactionary White Armies made extensive use of the Protocols to incite widespread slaughters of Jews."*[14] Two hundred thousand Jews were murdered in the Ukraine alone.

1920 The *Protocols* reach England and the United States. They are exposed as a forgery, but are widely circulated. Henry Ford [Ford Motor Company] sponsored a study of international activities of Jews. This led to a series of anti-Semitic articles in The *Dear born Independent,* which were published in a book, *"The International Jew."*

1920S,1930S **Hitler had published in *Mein Kampf* in 1925**, writing: *"Today I believe that I am acting in accordance with the will of the Almighty Creator: by defending myself against the Jew, I am fighting for the work of the Lord."* The *Protocols* were used by the Nazis to whip up public hatred of the Jews in the 1930's. Widespread pogroms occured in Greece, Hungary, Mexico, Poland, Rumania, and the USSR. Radio programs by many conservative American clergy, both Roman Catholic and Protestant, frequently attacked Jews. Reverend Fr. Charles E. Coughlin was one of the best known. *"In the 1930's, radio audiences heard him rail against the threat of Jews to America's economy and defend Hitler's treatment of Jews as justified in the fight against communism."*[15] Other conservative Christian leaders, such as Frank Norris and John Straton, supported the Jews.[16]

Discrimination against Jews in North America is widespread. Many universities set limits on the maximum number of Jewish students that they would accept. Harvard accepted all students on the basis of merit until after World War I when the percentage of Jewish students approached 15 percent. At that time they installed an informal quota system. In 1941, Princeton had fewer than 2 percent Jews in their student body. Jews were routinely barred from country clubs, prestigious neighborhoods, etc.[17]

1933 **Hitler took power in Germany**. On **April 1,** Julius Streicher organized a one-day boycott of all Jewish-owned businesses in the country. This was the start of continuous oppression by the Nazis, culminating in the Holocaust. Jews *"were barred from civil service, legal professions and universities, were not allowed to teach in schools and could not be editors of newspapers."*[18] Two years later, Jews were no longer considered citizens. Many Jews prefer to refer to the genocide of the World War II as the "Shoah"—which means 'calamity' in Hebrew (*Hashoah*). The word "Holocaust' comes from the Greek and means 'a completely *(holos) burnt (kaustos) sacrificial offering.' For many Jews it is theologically offensive to imply—by using the word Holocaust —that the European Jews were killed as a sacrifice to God. Nevertheless, it is widely recognized that most people do not intend such a meaning when they use the Greek word Holocaust.*

1934 Various laws were enacted in Germany to force Jews out of schools and professions.

1935 **The Nazis passed the *Nuremberg Laws*** restricting citizenship to those of "*German or related blood.*" Jews became stateless.

1938 On **November 9,** the Nazi government in Germany sent storm troopers, the SS and the Hitler Youth on a pogrom that killed 91 Jews, injured hundreds, burned 177 synagogues and looted 7,500 Jewish stores. Broken glass could be seen everywhere; the glass gave this event its name of Kristallnacht, the Night of Broken Glass.[19]

1939 *The Holocaust, the Shoah*—**the systematic extermination of Jews in Germany—begins. The process only ended in 1945 with the conclusion of World War II.** *Approximately 6 million Jews (1.5 million of them children), 400 thousand Roma (Gypsies) and others were slaughtered.* Some were killed by death squads; others were slowly killed in trucks with carbon monoxide; others were gassed in large groups in Auschwitz, Dachau, Sobibor, Treblinka and other extermination camps. Officially, the holocaust was described by the Nazis as subjecting Jews "*to special treatment*" or as a "*solution of the Jewish question.*" Gold taken from the teeth of the victims was recycled; hair was used in the manufacture of mattresses. In the Buchenwald extermination camp, lampshades were made out of human skin; however, this appears to be an isolated incident. A rumor spread that Jewish corpses were routinely converted into soap. However, the story appears to be false.[20]

1945 **The Shoah (Holocaust) ended as the Allied Forces overran the Nazi death camps.**

APPENDIX II

JEWRY AND ISRAEL REVIVAL CHART

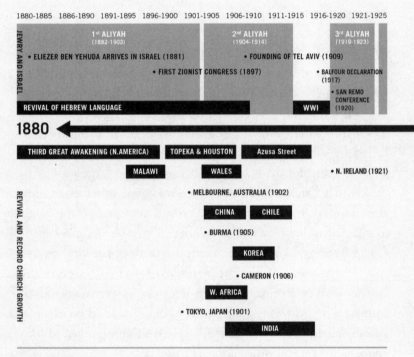

First Zionist Congress: Theodore Herzi convened inaugural Zionist Organization congress and established platform for modern Zionism.
Balfour Declaration: British gevernment endorses the establishment of a Jewish homeland in Palestine.
San Remo Conference: Allied powers confirmed the pledge of the Balfour Declaration.

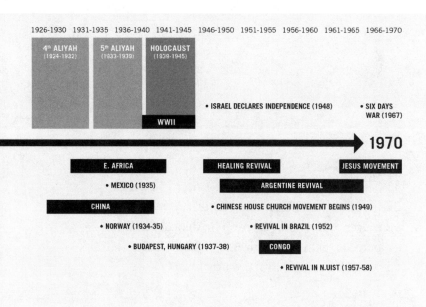

Topeka, KS & Houston, TX: Revival begins in Topeka with the Agnes Ozman speaking in tongues and spreads to Houston .

Azusa Street: Revival births the modern Pentecostal movement and an estimated 50,000 people receiving the gift of tongues.

Jesus Movement: Period of significant church growth and most notably a large number of Jewish believers added to the church.

APPENDIX III

JEWISH CONTRIBUTIONS TO HUMANITY

(Information provided courtesy of JINFO.org)

IN PHYSICS
51 percent of Wolf Foundation Prizes in Physics
28 percent of Max Planck Medailles
38 percent Dirac Medals for Theoretical Physics
37 percent Heineman Prizes for Mathematical Physics
53 percent Enrico Fermi Awards

IN PHILOSOPHY
30 percent of *Thinkers of the Twentieth Century*
37 percent of the Twenty-Seven "Most Important" Philosophical Works of the Twentieth Century
44 percent of the Fifty Most Frequently Cited Twentieth Century Works in the Arts & Humanities

IN MATHEMATICS

27 percent Fields Medalists

36 percent Wolf Prize in Mathematics

55 percent Leroy P. Steele Prize for Lifetime Achievement

44 percent Bocher Memorial Prize

40 percent Frank Nelson Cole Prize in Algebra and Number Theory

IN LITERATURE

14 percent Pulitzer Prize for Fiction

18 percent Pulitzer Prize for Poetry

53 percent Pulitzer Prize for Non-Fiction

34 percent Pulitzer Prize for Drama

41 percent Antoinette Perry (Tony) Award for Best Play

54 percent Antoinette Perry (Tony) Award for Best Book of a Musical

41 percent Academy Award for Best Original Screenplay

32 percent Academy Award for Best Adapted Screenplay

25 percent of the 250 Most Frequently Cited Authors (from antiquity to present) in the Arts & Humanities

44 percent of the 50 Most Frequently Cited Twentieth Century Works in the Arts & Humanities

IN COMPUTER AND INFORMATION SCIENCE

32 percent ACM A.M. Turing Award in Computer Science

36 percent IEEE C.E. Shannon Award in Information Technology

43 percent John von Neumann Theory Prize in Operations Research

45 percent EATCS /ACM Kurt Godel Prize in Theoretical

Computer Science
45 percent ACM Paris Kanellakis Theory & Practice Award in Computer Science
56 percent IMU Rolf Nevanlinna Prize in Computer & Information Science

MEDICINE
32 percent Lasker Award in Basic Medical Research
26 percent Gairdner Foundation Award
41 percent Wolf Prize in Medicine
40 percent Louise Gross Horwitz Prize
35 percent GM Cancer Research Foundation Sloan Prize

MUSIC
49 percent Academy Award for Best Original Song
49 percent Academy Award for Best Musical Scoring of a Musical Picture
69 percent Antoinette Perry (Tony) Award for Best Musical Production
70 percent Antoinette Perry (Tony) Award for Best Original Score of a Musical

APPENDIX IV

A SELECTED BIBLIOGRAPHY

Mitchell G. Bard. *Myths and Facts: A Guide to the Arab–Israeli Conflict.* Chevy Chase, MD: American Israeli Cooperative Enterprise, 2001.

Andrew G. Boston. *The Legacy of Jihad: Islamic Holy War and the Fate of Non Muslims.* Amherst, NY: Prometheus Books, 2008.

Michael L. Brown. *Our Hands are Stained with Blood.* Shippensburg, PA: Destiny Image, 1992.

George Gilder. *The Israel Test.* Minneapolis: Richard Vigilante Books, 2009.

Doug Hershey. *The Christians Biblcial Guide to Understanding Israel.* Lake Mary, FL: Creation House Books, 2011.

Daniel Juster. *Jewish Roots: Understanding Your Jewish Faith.* Shippensburg, PA: Destiny Image, 2013.

Daniel Juster. *The Irrevocable Calling: Israel's Role as a Light to the Nations.* Clarksville, MD: Lederer Books, 2007.

Miriam Rodlyn Park. *Watchmen on the Wall: A Practical Guide to Prayer for Jerusalem and Her People.* Clarence, NY: Kairos, 2008.

Michael Prell. *Underdogma: How America's Enemies Use Our Love for the Underdog to Trash American Power.* Dallas: BenBella Books, 2011.

Robert Stearns. *Cry of Mordecai.* Shippensburg, PA: Destiny Image, 2009.

Robert Stearns. *No We Can't: Radical Islam, Militant Secularism, and the Myth of Coexistence.* Bloomington, MN: Chosen Books, 2011.

Sandra Teplinsky. *Why Still Care About Israel?* Bloomington: Chosen Books, 2004, 2013.
Cynthia D. Wallace. *Foundations of the International Legal Rights of the Jewish People and the State of Israel.* Lake Mary: Creation House, 2012.

Marvin R. Wilson. *Our Father Abraham: Jewish Roots of the Christian Faith.* Grand Rapids: Eerdmans, 1989.

Bat Ye'or. *The Decline of Eastern Christianity under Isalm: From Jihad to Dhimmitude Seven-Twentieth Century.* Cranbury, NJ: Associated University Presses, 1996.

NOTES

CHAPTER 1: JESUS' STORY

1. "Bible Engagement in Churchgoers' Hearts Not Always Practiced," LifeWay Research, November 15, 2013, http://www.lifewayresearch.com/2013/11/15/bible-engagement-in-churchgoers-hearts-not-always-practiced-2/.

2. Ed Stetzer, "Dumb and Dumber: How Biblical Illiteracy Is Killing Our Nation," *Charisma* magazine, October 9, 2014, http://www.charismamag.com/life/culture/21076-dumb-and-dumber-how-biblical-illiteracy-is-killing-our-nation.

3. Ibid.

4. Marvin R. Wilson, *Our Father Abraham: Jewish Roots of the Christian Faith* (Grand Rapids: Eerdmans, 1989), 112.

5. *Catechism of the Catholic Church*, 2nd ed., 121.

6. "354 Prophecies Fulfilled in Jesus Christ," According to the Scriptures, January 20, 2015, http://www.accordingtothescriptures.org/prophecy/353prophecies.html.

7. Daniel Juster, *Jewish Roots: Understanding Your Jewish Faith* (Shippensburg, PA: Destiny Image, 2013), 93.

8. Stetzer, "Dumb and Dumber."

9. Juster, *Jewish Roots*, 93.

CHAPTER 2: A FAMILY AFFAIR

1. Derek Prince, *Why Israel?* (teaching CD, track 1, 2:15), © 1998 Derek Prince Ministries.

2. John Adams, letter to F. A. Vanderkemp, February 16, 1809.

3. See Thomas Edward McComiskey, *The Covenants of Promise: A Theology of the Old Testament Covenants* (n.p.: Baker Book House Company, 1985), 59.

4. See Daniel Juster, *Jewish Roots: Understanding Your Jewish Faith* (Shippensburg, PA: Destiny Image, 2013), 61; and McComiskey, *The Covenants of Promise*, 91–92.

5. See David Parsons, *Swords into Ploughshares: Christian Zionism and the Battle of Armageddon* (International Christian Embassy Jerusalem), 20–23, http://int.icej.org/sites/default/files/en/pdf/Swords%20into%20Ploughshares.pdf.

6. Ibid., 20.

7. Juster, *Jewish Roots*, 91.

8. Wayne Grudem, *Bible Doctrine: Essential Teachings of the Christian Faith* (Grand Rapids: Zondervan, 1999), 76–77.

9. Mark Twain, "Concerning the Jews," *Harper's Magazine*, September 1899Twain, Reprinted in Scott, Horton, "The Unwanted Immigrant, *Harper's Magazine*, June 10, 2007. http://harpers.org/blog/2007/06/the-unwanted-immigrant/.

10. George Gilder, "Capitalism, Jewish Achievement, and the Israel Test," *The American*, July 27, 2009, American Enterprise Institute, https://www.aei.org/publication/capitalism-jewish-achievement-and-the-israel-test/.

11. "Jews Listed Among the Creators of the Greatest Lifesaving Medical and Scientific Advances in History," JINFO.org, accessed July 10, 2015, http://www.jinfo.org/Life_Savers.html.

12. "Israel on the frontline of international aid," Israel Ministry of Foreign Affairs, accessed July 10, 2015, http://www.mfa.gov.il/MFA/ForeignPolicy/Aid/Pages/Israel_humanitarian_aid.aspx.

13. "Israel's aid team to Nepal among the largest," The Times of Israel, April 29, 2015, http://www.timesofisrael.com/israels-aid-team-to-nepal-larger-than-any-other-countrys/.

14. *Israel Innovations* (Los Angeles: StandWithUs, 2014), http://www.standwithus.com/booklets/innovations/.

15. Thomas Cahill, *The Gift of the Jews: How a Tribe of Desert Nomads Changed the Way Everyone Thinks and Feels* (New York: Nan A. Talese, 1998), 3.

16. See Marvin R. Wilson, *Our Father Abraham: Jewish Roots of the Christian Faith* (Grand Rapids: Eerdmans, 1989), 246.

17. Michael Oren, *Power, Faith, and Fantasy: America in the Middle East 1776 to the Present* (New York: W. W. Norton, 2007), 369.

18. Great Britain, Parliamentary Papers, *Palestine: Statement of Policy* (London: His Majesty's Stationery Office, 1939), 195.

19. Raymond L. Ganon, *The Shifting Romance with Israel* (Shippensburg, PA: Destiny Image, 2012), 52.

20. Gary B. McGee, "1901—The Holy Spirit Falls at Topeka," Foundations in Christianity, accessed July 10, 2015, http://www.foundationsinchristianity.org/1901_The_Holy_Spirit_Falls_at_Topeka.htm.

21. Ganon, *The Shifting Romance with Israel*, 21.

22. "Interview with Abd al-Rahman Azzam Pasha," *Akhbar al-Yom* (Egypt), October 11, 1947; translated by R. Green.

23. Michael Oren, *Six Days of War: June 1967 and the Making of the Modern Middle East* (New York: Random House, 2003), xii.

24. For more on this topic, see D. E. Harrell, *All Things Are Possible: The Healing and Charismatic Revivals in Modern America* (Indiana University Press, 1978); R. H. Krapohl and C. H. Lippy, *The Evangelicals: A Historical, Thematic, and Biographical Guide* (Westport, CT: Greenwood Press, 1999); and W. J. Hollenweger, *Pentecostalism: Origins and Developments Worldwide* (Peabody, MA: Hendrickson, 1997).

25. For more on this topic, see David Di Sabatino, *The Jesus People Movement: An Annotated Bibliography and General Resource* (Westport, CT: Greenwood Press, 1999); Jean Duchesne, *Jesus Revolution: Made in U.S.A.* (Paris: Éditions du Cerf, 1972); Billy Graham, *The Jesus Generation* (Grand Rapids, MI: Zondervan, 1971), Edward E. Plowman, *The Jesus Movement* (London: Hodder and Stoughton, 1972); and Shawn David Young, *Hippies, Jesus Freaks, and Music* (Ann Arbor: Xanedu/Copley Original Works, 2005).

26. The word *Tel* is an archaeological term referring to a city that's built on multiple layers of previous civilizations; *Aviv* is a spring; Tel-Aviv literally means "hill of the spring." However, the name is taken from the Hebrew title of Theodor Herzl's book *Altneuland* (Old-New Land).

CHAPTER 3: WHOSE STORY ARE YOU IN?

1. See Rick Warren, Daniel Amen, and Mark Hyman, *The Daniel Plan: 40 Days to a Healthier Life* (Grand Rapids: Zondervan, 2013); and the Daniel Plan website: https://www.danielplan.com/start/.

2. Charles Duhigg, *The Power of Habit: Why We Do What We Do In Life and Business* (New York: Random House, 2012), 234–35.

3. Jonathan Sacks, *Future Tense: Jews, Judaism, and Israel in the Twenty-First Century* (New York: Random House, 2009), 75.

4. A. W. Tozer, *The Knowledge of the Holy* (New York: HarperCollins, 1961), 98.

5. Elie Wiesel, *The Gates of the Forest* (Austin[?]: Holt, Rinehart and Winston, 1966).

6. Frank McLynn, *1759: The Year Britain Became Master of the World* (New York: Atlantic Monthly Press, 2004), 35.

7. World Digital Library, s.v. "The Battle of the Monongahela," accessed July 20, 2015, http://www.wdl.org/en/item/9580/.

8. Matthew C. Ward, "Fighting the 'old Women,'" *Virginia Magazine of History and Biography*, 1995, 297.

9. Fred Anderson, *Crucible of War: The Seven Years' War and the Fate of Empire in British North America, 1754–1766* (New York: Alfred A. Knopf, 2000), 102.

10. James Hadden, *Washington's Expedition (1753–1754) and Braddock's Expedition (1755)* (Uniontown: James Hadden, 1910), 117.

11. Anderson, *Crucible of War*, 103–4

12. George Washington, *George Washington: Writings,* ed. John H. Rhodehamel (Literary Classics of the United States, 1997), 59–60.

13. Marvin R. Wilson, *Our Father Abraham: Jewish Roots of the Christian Faith* (Grand Rapids: Eerdmans, 1989), 112.

CHAPTER 4: HATRED THAT PASSES UNDERSTANDING

1. The White House, Office of the Press Secretary, "Press Conference by President Obama and President Yudhoyono of Indonesia in Jakarta, Indonesia," November 9, 2010, https://www.whitehouse.gov/the-press-office/2010/11/09/press-conference-president-obama-and-president-yudhoyono-indonesia-jakar.

2. "Indonesia Population," Worldometers, live as of July 1, 2014, http://www.worldometers.info/world-population/indonesia-population/.

3. BBC, "BBC World Service Poll," May 22, 2013, accessed February 22, 2015, http://www.worldpublicopinion.org/pipa/2013%20Country%20Rating%20Poll.pdf.

4. Sharon Udasin, "Israel Passes US, Europe in Bottle Recycling," *Jerusalem Post*, March 15, 2012, http://www.jpost.com/Enviro-Tech/Israel-passes-US-Europe-in-bottle-recycling.

5. "Waste Facts and Figures," Israel Ministry of Environmental Protection, upd. May 17, 2015, http://www.sviva.gov.il/English/env_topics/Solid_Waste/FactsAndFigures/Pages/default.aspx.

6. "Egypt," Sweepnet, accessed July 15, 2015, http://www.sweep-net.org/country/egypt.

7. Sweepnet, *Country Report on the Solid Waste Management in Jordan* April 2014

8. Andrey Kastelmacher, "Vast Solar Roof Makes Israeli Knesset World's Greenest Parliament," NoCamels, April 13, 2015, http://nocamels.com/2015/04/solar-roof-israeli-knesset-greenest-parliament/.

9. David Shamah, "Israeli Water Tech Reaching America's Biggest States," *Times of Israel*, March 9, 2014, http://www.timesofisrael.com/israeli-water-tech-reaching-americas-biggest-states/.

10. JTA, "Philly Mayor to Officiate Same-Sex Marriage for Israeli Diplomat," *Forward*, January 13, 2015, http://forward.com/news/breaking-news/212629/philly-mayor-to-officiate-same-sex-marriage-for-is/.

11. Ramon Johnson, "What About Gays in North Korea?" *About Relationships,* accessed March, 15 2015, http://gaylife.about.com/od/samesexmarriage/qt/gaykorea.htm.

12. StandWithUs, "LGBT Rights in Israel and the Middle East," 2015, http://www.standwithus.com/booklets/LGBT/.

13. Article 6.21 of the Russian Federation on Administrative Offenses, https://lgbtnet.ru/sites/default/files/russian_federal_draft_law_on_propaganda_of_non-traditional_sexual_relations_2d_reading_eng.pdf.

14. The Druze are an offshoot of Islam originating in Egypt in the eleventh century, but they don't consider themselves Muslim. Druze communities can be found in Israel, Jordan, Syri,a and Lebanon.

15. Linda Gradstein, "More Bedouin Women Turn to Academia," Ynet News, October 21, 2013, http://www.ynetnews.com/articles/0,7340,L-4443176,00.html.

16. Steven Jagord, "Israeli Woman Shares Minority Experience," *Clarence Bee*, November 27, 2013, http://www.clarencebee.com/news/2013-11- 27/Front_Page/Israeli_woman_shares_minority_experience.html.

17. *The Global Gender Gap Report 2014* (Geneva: World Economic Forum, 2014), http://www.weforum.org/reports/global-gender-gap-report-2014, 8–9.

18. "Women's Rights Country by Country—Interactive," *Guardian* (UK), February 4, 2014, http://www.theguardian.com/global-development/ng-interactive/2014/feb/04/womens-rights-country-by-country-interactive.

19. StandWithUs, "LGBT Rights in Israel and the Middle East."

20. Jerusalem Institute of Justice, *Hidden Injustices: A Review of Palestinian Authority and Hamas Human Rights Violations in the West Bank and Gaza* (March 2015), 32, http://jij.org.il/wp-content/uploads/2013/10/Hidden-Injustices.-Human-Rights-in-the-PA-7.4.13.pdf.

21. Beenish Ahmed, "Telling the Stories of the Victims of 'Honor Killings,'" ThinkProgress, June 17, 2015, http://thinkprogress.org/world/2015/06/17/3670460/honor-crimes/.

22. Farhana Qzai, "America's Honor Killings a Growing Reality," *Islamic Monthly*, June 30, 2014, http://theislamicmonthly.com/americas-honor-killings-a-growing-reality/.

23. David Brog, *Standing with Israel: Why Christians Support the Jewish State* (Lake Mary: Frontline, 2006), 92–97.

24. Theodor Herzl, *The Jewish State* (New York: Dover, 1988), 146.

25. "THE STATE OF ISRAEL will be open for Jewish immigration and for the Ingathering of the Exiles; it will foster the development of the country for the benefit of all its inhabitants; it will be based on freedom, justice and peace as envisaged by the prophets of Israel; it will ensure complete equality of social and political rights to all its inhabitants irrespective of religion, race or sex; it will guarantee freedom of religion, conscience, language, education and culture; it will safeguard the Holy Places of all religions; and it will be faithful to the principles of the Charter of the United Nations." ("Declaration of Establishment of State of Israel," May 14, 1948, Israel Ministry of Foreign Affairs, accessed August 15, 2015, http://www.mfa.gov.il/mfa/foreignpolicy/peace/guide/pages/declaration%20of%20establishment%20of%20state%20of%20israel.aspx.)

26. Moshe Dayan, *Moshe Dayan: Story of My Life* (New York: William Morrow, 1976), 387–90.

27. Contrary to the current revisionist history of the Temple Mount, the visitor's guide for the Temple Mount produced and sold by the Supreme Moslem Council in 1924 recognizes the site of the Temple Mount as the location of the temple and refers to it as, "beyond dispute." For more information visit, TempleMountGuide.com.

28. Lahav Harkov, "Arabs harass US congressmen during visit to Temple Mount," *Jerusalem Post*, August 11, 2015, http://m.jpost.com/Arab-Israeli-Conflict/Exclusive-Muslims-harass-Congressmen-visiting-Temple-Mount-411782#article=6024OTI2MEMzRD E2OTUyNzlDQjhCNUFFQTQzQkY2MzMxNkY=.

29. "2002 Basic Law," Palestinian Basic Law, Article 4, accessed August 10, 2015, http://www.palestinianbasiclaw.org/basic-law/2002-basic-law.

30. "Backgrounder: The PA's treatment of Christians," *Middle East Digest*, November–December 1997.

31. Arlene Kushner, *Disclosed: Inside the Palestinian Authority and the PLO* (Philadelphia: Pavilion Press, 2004), 93–94.

32. Jerusalem Institute of Justice, *Hidden Injustices: A Review of Palestinian Authority and Hamas Human Rights Violations in the West Bank and Gaza* (November, 2012), 24. http://jij.org.il/wp-content/uploads/2013/10/Hidden-Injustices.-Human-Rights-in-the-PA-7.4.13.pdf.

33. Ibid., 32.

34. Richard Goldstone, "Israel and the Apartheid Slander" *New York Times*, October 31, 2011, http://www.nytimes.com/2011/11/01/opinion/israel-and-the-apartheid-slander.html.

35. As early as 1919 Haj Amin al-Husseini, grand mufti of Jerusalem, had begun to form small groups of *fedayeen* (suicide fighters) to terrorize Jewish communities. In April 1920, fedayeen and Arab communities rioted in response to the San Remo meeting of the Allies; San Remo laid the legal foundation for a Jewish Homeland. Riots resulted in six Jewish deaths and two hundred wounded.

36. Rising tensions due, in part, to increased Jewish immigration and Arab propaganda spiked in August 1929. Arab mobs formed in the city of Hebron, and on August 23, 1929, sixty-seven Jews were murdered.

37. The British White Paper of 1939 recognizes Arab terrorism: "The lamentable disturbances of the past three years are only the latest and most sustained manifestation of this intense Arab apprehension. The methods employed by Arab terrorists against fellow Arabs and Jews alike must receive unqualified condemnation," section 2, available on the website of the Avalon Project, accessed October 23, 2015, http://avalon.law.yale.edu/20th_century/brwh1939.asp.

38. "Over 111 terrorist attacks stopped in West Bank, Jerusalem in 2015," JTA, August 13, 2015, http://www.jta.org/2015/08/13/news-opinion/israel-middle-east/over-111-terror-attacks-stopped-in-west-bank-jerusalem-in-2015.

39. "Egypt's Wall of Shame," *Tripoli Post*, December 27, 2009, http://www.tripolipost.com/articledetail.asp?c=1&i=3902.

40. Calev Myers & The Whole Story Project: The Wall? Israel's response to Palestinian terror," You Tube, 3:02, posted by Jerusalem Institute of Justice, accessed December 7, 2015, https://www.youtube.com/watch?v=2ph9g39muwo.

41. "Over 111 terrorist attacks stopped in West Bank."

42. "Female Israeli Soldier Wounded in Stabbing at Checkpoint Near Bethlehem," Haaretz, June 28, 2015, http://www.haaretz.com/news/diplomacy-defense/.premium-1.663489.

43. "Vital Statistics: Total Casualties, Arab–Israeli Conflict," Jewish Virtual Library, accessed February 5, 2015, http://www.jewishvirtuallibrary.org/jsource/History/casualtiestotal.html.

44. "Table 1.2: 20th Century Democide," accessed July 27, 2015, http://www.hawaii.edu/powerkills/DBG.TAB1.2.GIF.

45. Neil Maclucas, "U.N. Says Syria Deaths Near 200,000," *Wall Street Journal*, August 22, 2014, http://www.wsj.com/articles/u-n-says-syria-deaths-near-200-000-1408697916.

46. Max Fisher, "More Syrians have died in 3 years of war than Americans in every war since WW2," Vox, August 26, 2014, http://www.vox.com/2014/8/26/6056605/syria-fatalities-comparisons.

47. "What Was the 1970 Jordanian–Palestinian Conflict Known as 'Black September'?" ProCon.org, February 22, 2012, http://israelipalestinian.procon.org/view.answers.php?questionID=000435.

48. "Vital Statistics: Total Casualties, Arab–Israeli Conflict.

49. *Wall Street Journal* (February 21, 1990), quoted by Mitchell G. Bard, *Myths and Facts: A Guide to the Arab-Israeli Conflict* (Chevy Chase: American Israeli Cooperative Enterprise, 2001), 246.

50. Ibid. (A "succah" is a temporary shelter constructed during the celebration of the Feast of Tabernacles.)

51. Paul Robert Magocsi, *Historical Atlas of East Central Europe* (Seattle: University of Washington Press, 1993) 165–68.

52. United Nations High Commissioner for Refugees, "Rupture in South Asia" (chap. 3), *State of the World's Refugees 2000* (UNCHR), accessed August 8, 2015, http://www.unhcr.org/3ebf9bab0.pdf.

53. "Main Facts: Displacement of Jews from Arab Countries 1928–2012," Justice for Jews from Arab Countries, accessed August 8, 2015, http://www.justiceforjews.com/main_facts.html.

54. "Cambodia: A Decade of War and Forced Migration," Columbia University, accessed August 8, 2015, http://forcedmigration.ccnmtl.columbia.edu/book/export/html/25.

55. "2015 UNHCR country operations profile – Sudan," UNHCR, accessed November 30, 2015, http://www.unhcr.org/pages/49e483b76.html.

56. "Turkey: internal displacement in brief," Internal Displacement Monitoring Centre, December 31, 2013, http://www.internal-displacement.org/europe-the-caucasus-and-central-asia/turkey/summary.

57. Steven J. Rosen, "Kuwait Expels Thousands of Palestinians," *Middle East Quarterly*, 2012, 75–83, http://www.meforum.org/3391/kuwait-expels-palestinians.

58. Hassan A. El-Najjar, "Palestinians in Kuwait: Terror and Ethnic Cleansing," in *The Gulf War: Overreaction and Excessiveness* (Dalton, GA: Amazone Press, 2001), chap. 10, Table X.2 quoted in ibid.

59. Daniel Pipes, "The Hell of Israel Is Better Than the Paradise of Arafat," *Middle East Quarterly*, Spring 2005, 43–50, quoted in ibid.

60. "The Rwandan Genocide" History, accessed November 15, 2015, http://www.history.com/topics/rwandan-genocide.

61. "Israel's Disengagement from Gaza and North Samaria (2005)" Israel Ministry of Foreign Affairs, accessed August 8, 2015, http://www.mfa.gov.il/mfa/aboutisrael/maps/pages/israels%20disengagement%20plan-%202005.aspx.

62. "A Snapshot of the Crisis—in the Middle East and Europe," Syrian Refugees, accessed August 8, 2015, http://syrianrefugees.eu/.

63. Friends of Israel Initiative, "Yarmouk falls into oblivion," *Dispatch* 22, April 2015, http://www.friendsofisraelinitiative.org/uploads/alerts/pdfs/28.pdf, p. 2.

64. Mindy Blez, "In the Shadow of ISIS," *World,* August 22, 2015, 48.

65. Information provided courtesy of the Jerusalem Institute of Justice. Also see, "Disturbing: How We Are Financing the Suffering of the Palestinians," You Tube, 3:40, posted by Jerusalem Institute of Justice, accessed December 7, 2015, https://www.youtube.com/watch?v=m5YPCenFVS0.

66. Four million represents the Palestinian population at the time of these calculations.

67. The Palestinian Liberation Organization (PLO) was created in 1964 to officially represent the Palestinian people. The PLO has taken credit for terrorist attacks on Israelis and Americans. Until 1991 the PLO was classified by the United States as a terrorist organization.

68. Rachel Ehrenfeld, "The Palestinian Authority: Where Does the Money Go?" American Center for Democracy, October 2002; and Ronen Bergman, "How Much is the PLO really worth?" Ha'aretz, November 28, 1999, quoted in Arlene Kushner, *Disclosed: Inside the Palestinian Authority and the PLO* (Philadelphia: Pavilion Press, 2004), 72.

69. Doron Peskin, "Hamas got rich as Gaza was plunged into poverty," YNet News, Business & Finance, July 15, 2014, http://www.ynetnews.com/articles/0,7340,L-4543634,00.html.

70. Michael Prell, *Underdogma: How America's Enemies Use Our Love for the Underdog to Trash American Power* (Dallas: BenBella Books, 2011).

71. "Defining Palestine and the Palestinians," DiscoverTheNetworks.org, accessed October 23, 2015, http://www.discoverthenetworks.org/viewSubCategory.asp?id=46.

72. Jordan is the only Arab country to grant citizenship to Palestinians.

73. Friends of Israel Initiative, "Yarmouk falls into oblivion."

74. Staff Writer, "'Return' as Weapon to Destroy Israel," *Jewish Post,* accessed October 23, 2015, http://www.jewishpost.com/archives/news/return-as-weapon-to-destroy-israel.html.

75. Ibid.

76. The British White Paper of 1939 recognizes Jewish accomplishment prior to 1948, "The growth of the Jewish National Home and its achievements in many fields are a remarkable constructive effort which must command the admiration of the world," section 1.

77. "UN, Israel & Anti-Semitism," UN Watch, 2015, accessed August 8, 2015, http://www.unwatch.org/site/c.bdKKISNqEmG/b.1359197/k.6748/UN_Israel__AntiSemitism.htm, no longer accessible.

78. "Calev Myers on Understanding UN Bias Against Israel, The Jerusalem Institute of Justice," YouTube video, 3:55, posted by the Jerusalem Institute of Justice, July 12, 2011, https://www.youtube.com/watch?v=j7Mupoo1At8.

79. For more on international law regarding Israel, see: Cynthia D. Wallace, *Foundations of the International Legal Rights of the Jewish People and the State of Israel* (Lake Mary: Creation House, 2012); and Jacques Paul Gauthier, *Sovereignty over the Old City of Jerusalem: A Study of the Historical, Religious, Political and Legal Aspects of the Question of the Old City,* Thesis no.725 (University of Geneva, 2007).

CHAPTER 5: REFLECTIONS OF THE INVISIBLE

1. Donald E. Gowan, *Daniel* (Nashville: Abingdon Press, 2001), 141.

2. Gleason L. Archer Jr., *The Expositor's Bible Commentary*, vol. 7, *Daniel*, gen. ed. Frank E. Gaebelein (Grand Rapids: Zondervan, 1990), 125.

3. See Clinton E. Arnold, *Powers of Darkness: Principalities & Powers in Paul's Letters* (Downers Grove, IL: InterVarsity Press, 1992), 202.

4. For more on this topic, see Robert Stearns, *Keepers of the Flame* (Clarence, NY: Kairos, 2003).

5. Robert Webber, *The Church in the World: Opposition, Tension, or Transformation?* (Grand Rapids: Zondervan, 1986), 14–15.

6. Arnold, *Powers of Darkness*, 196–97.

7. See Watchmen Nee, *The Spiritual Man*, vol. 1 (New York: Christian Fellowship Publishers, 1977), 86.

8. Eyal Zisser, "Iranian Involvement in Lebanon," *Military and Strategic Affairs* 3, no. 1 (May 2011): 3, http://www.inss.org.il/uploadImages/systemFiles/MASA%20-%203.1.pdf.

9. For more on this topic see, Robert Stearns, *No We Can't: Radical Islam, Militant Secularism, and the Myth of Coexistence* (Bloomington, MN: Chosen Books, 2011).

10. Daniel C. Juster, "Anti-Semitism Again," *Jewish Voice Today Magazine,* July/August/September 2015.

11. Albert Lee, *Henry Ford and the Jews* (New York: Stein and Day, 1980), 14.

12. "Interview: Ford's Anti-Semitism," PBS, accessed July 27, 2015, http://www.pbs.org/wgbh/americanexperience/features/interview/henryford-antisemitism/.

13. "About," ADL Global 100, accessed July 27, 2015, http://global100.adl.org/#map/2015update.

14. "Iraq," ADL Global 100, accessed July 27, 2015, http://global100.adl.org/#country/iraq.

15. Anti-Defamation League, *Islamic Anti-Semitism in Historical Perspective* (2002), 8, http://archive.adl.org/anti_semitism/arab/arab_anti-semitism.pdf.

CHAPTER 6: A FAMILY FEUD

1. For more on Christian anti-Semitism see, Michael L. Brown, *Our Hands are Stained with Blood* (Shippensburg, PA: Destiny Image, 1992).
2. Daniel Juster, *Jewish Roots: Understanding Your Jewish Faith* (Shippensburg: Destiny Image, 2013), 182–83.
3. Sandra Teplinsky, *Why Still Care About Israel?* (Bloomington: Chosen Books, 2004, 2013), 49.
4. David Max Eichhorn, *Evangelizing the American Jew* (Middle Village: Jonathan David, 1978), 6.
5. John Owen, *The Works of John Owen*, vol.17 (Carlisle, PA: The Banner of Truth Trust, 1850, 2004), exercitation 18, 560.
6. Juster, *Jewish Roots*, 196.
7. Dennis M. Swanson, *Charles H. Spurgeon and the Nation of Israel*, The Spurgeon Archive, 2000, accessed January 19, 2015, http://www.spurgeon.org/misc/eschat2.htm.
8. Robert Stearns, *Cry of Mordecai* (Shippensburg, PA: Destiny Image, 2009).
9. Jonathan Sacks, *Future Tense: Jews, Judaism, and Israel in the Twenty-First Century* (New York: Random House, 2009), 92–98.
10. See Sandra Teplinsky, *Why Still Care About Israel?* (Bloomington: Chosen Books, 2004, 2013), 125.
11. Gary M. Burge, *Whose Land? Whose Promise?: What Christians Are Not Being Told about Israel and the Palestinians* (Cleveland: Pilgrim Press, 2003), 1.
12. Naim Stifan Ateek, *Justice and Only Justice: A Palestinian Theology of Liberation* (Maryknoll, NY: Orbis Books, 1991), 79.
13. Ibid., 22.
14. Ibid., 1.
15. Burge, *Whose Land? Whose Promise?*, 7.
16. "Reform Judaism: The Tenets of Reform Judaism," Jewish Virtual Library, accessed May 5, 2015, http://www.jewishvirtuallibrary.org/jsource/Judaism/reform_practices.html#Messiah; and Elaine Rose Glickman, *The Messianic Concept in Reform Judaism*, My Jewish Learning, accessed May 5, 2015, http://www.myjewishlearning.com/article/the-messianic-concept-in-reform-judaism/2/.
17. Walter C. Kaiser Jr., *To The Jew First: The Case for Jewish Evangelism in Scripture and History*, ed. Darrell L. Bock and Mitch Glaser (Grand Rapids: Kregel, 2008), 52.

CHAPTER 7: "WHAT IS IT TO YOU? FOLLOW ME!"

1. Avi Baumol, *The Israel Bible: The Book of Psalms* (Ramat Beit Shemesh, Israel: Israel365, 2014), 206.
2. Ibid.
3. John Piper, *Think: The Life of the Mind and the Love of God* (Wheaton, IL: Crossway, 2010).

4. Daniel Juster, *Jewish Roots: Understanding Your Jewish Faith* (Shippensburg, PA: Destiny Image, 2013), 57.
5. See Sandra Teplinsky, *Why Still Care About Israel?* (Bloomington, MN: Chosen Books, 2004, 2013), 89–90; and Daniel Juster, *Irrevocable Calling.* (Clarksville, MD: Messianic Jewish Publishers, 1996, 2007).
6. *Catechism of the Catholic Church*, 2nd ed., 839.
7. *Catechism of the Catholic Church*, 2nd ed., 218.
8. *Catechism of the Catholic Church*, 2nd ed., 674.

CHAPTER 8: WILD BLESSING

1. "Jerusalem Architectural History: British Mandate Period," Jewish Virtual Library, accessed July 27, 2015, https://www.jewishvirtuallibrary.org/jsource/Archaeology/jermandate.html.
2. See Miriam Rodlyn Park, *Watchmen on the Wall: A Practical Guide to Prayer for Jerusalem and Her People* (Clarence, NY: Kairos, 2008), 60–67.
3. See Steven N. Khoury, *Diplomatic Christianity: Standing in the Shadow of Tomorrow's Persecution* (Jerusalem: HMC Press, 2008), 31–46.
4. See Marvin R. Wilson, *Our Father Abraham: Jewish Roots of the Christian Faith* (Grand Rapids: Eerdmans, 1989), 275; and Jack W. Hayford, "Why Stand With Israel Today," *Jewish Voice Today Magazine,* July/August/September 2015.
5. Concept taken from Doug Hershey, author of *The Christian's Biblical Guide to Understanding Israel,* in a presentation for Eagles' Wings Watchmen on the Wall seminars.
6. See Job 6:5; 11:12; 24:5; 39:5; Ps. 104:11; Isa. 32:14; Jer. 2:24; 14:6; Hos. 8:9.
7. Sandra Teplinsky, *Why Still Care About Israel?* (Bloomington, MN: Chosen Books, 2004, 2013), 82–84.
8. Concept taken from Hershey, Watchmen presentation.
9. *The Amplified Bible* (Grand Rapids: Zondervan, 1987), 15.
10. Adolf Hitler, *Mein Kampf,* vol. 2, chap. 13 (1925), available online at http://www.mondopolitico.com/library/meinkampf/v2c13.htm.
11. James Pool, *Who Financed Hitler: The Secret Funding of Hitler's Power,* in John Simkin, "*Mein Kampf*: Nazi Germany," Spartacus Educational, August 2014, http://spartacus-educational.com/GERmein.htm.
12. See Robert Stearns, *Cry of Mordecai* (Shippensburg, PA: Destiny Image, 2009).
13. Adolf Hitler, *Mein Kampf* (New York: Houghton Mifflin, 1971), 324–25.
14. Max Domarus, *The Complete Hitler: A Digital Desktop Reference to His Speeches and Proclamations, 1932–1945* (Mundelein, IL: Bolchazy-Carducci, 1990), 1638.
15. Gilbert Achcar, *The Arabs and the Holocaust: The Arab–Israeli War of Narratives* (New York: Henry Holt, 2009), 125–26.
16. Communique, December 8, 1941, in Domarus, *The Complete Hitler,* 2530–31.

17. Communique, July 17, 1942) in ibid., 2652.

18. Teplinsky, *Why Still Care About Israel*, 176–77.

19. In 1933 Germany was 67 percent Protestant and 33 percent Catholic.

20. John Simkin, "Adolf Hitler: 1924–1932," Spartacus Educational, June 2015, http://spartacus-educational.com/GERhitler2.htm.

21. Albert Speer, *Inside the Third Reich: Memoirs* (New York: Simon & Schuster, 1970), 96.

22. Andrew G. Boston, *The Legacy of Jihad: Islamic Holy War and the Fate of Non-Muslims* (Amherst, NY: Prometheus Books, 2008), 29.

23. See, Bat Ye'or, *The Decline of Eastern Christianity under Isalm: From Jihad to Dhimmitude Seven-Twentieth Century* (Cranbury, NJ: Associated University Presses, 1996) and *The Dhimmi: Jews and Christians under Islam* (Madison, NJ: Fairleigh Dickinson University Press, 1985).

24. Arthur Jeffery, "The Political Importance of Islam," *Journal of Near Eastern Studies* 1 (1942): 386, in Boston, *The Legacy of Jihad*, 24.

25. Sarah Berger, "Christians Joining the Israel Defence Forces at Record Rates; Military Training Includes Visits to Jerusalem," *International Business Times*, August 7, 2015, http://www.ibtimes.com/christians-joining-israel-defense-forces-record-rates-military-training-includes-2044571#.VciOmd2sVIU.mailto.

26. Jerusalem Institute of Justice, *Hidden Injustices: A Review of Palestinian Authority and Hamas Human Rights Violations in the West Bank and Gaza*, March 2015, 24; http://jij.org.il/wp-content/uploads/2013/10/Hidden-Injustices.-Human-Rights-in-the-PA-7.4.13.pdf.

27. Reuters, "Gunmen killed 6 alleged collaborators in Gaza," Ma'an News Agency, November 20, 2012, http://www.maannews.com/Content.aspx?id=540228.

28. Arlene Kushner, *Disclosed: Inside the Palestinian Authority and the PLO* (Philadelphia: Pavilion Press, 2004), 137–38.

29. The Independent Commission for Human Rights, *The Status of Human Rights in Palestine: Twentieth Annual Report, 1 January–31 December 2014*, accessed July 15, 2015, http://www.ichr.ps/en/2/6/1360/ICHR-20th-Annual-Report-ICHR-20th-Annual-Report.htm, p. 8.

30. "Calev Myers on the Israeli Palestinian Conflict: 10 Myths Preventing Peace," You Tube, 5:45, posted by Jerusalem Institute of Justice, accessed December 7, 2015, https://www.youtube.com/watch?v=GdtGOY8T5XE.

31. Teplinsky, *Why Still Care About Israel?*, 179.

32. Folke Bernadotte, *To Jerusalem* (London: Hodder and Stoughton, 1951), 113.

33. George Gilder, *The Israel Test* (Minneapolis: Richard Vigilante Books, 2009), 49.

34. Ibid., 49–50.

35. Arieh Avneri, *The Claim of Dispossession* (Tel Aviv: Hidekel Press, 1984), 254, in Mitchell G. Bard, *Myths and Facts: A Guide to the Arab–Israeli Conflict* (Chevy Chase, MD: American Israeli Cooperative Enterprise, 2001), 43.

36. Moshe Auman, "Land Ownership in Palestine 1880–1948," in Michael Curtis et al., *The Palestinians,* (n.p.: Transaction Books, 1975), 38, quoted by Bard, *Myths and Facts,* 43.

37. Avneri, *The Claim of Dispossession,* 264; and Aharon Cohen, *Israel and the Arab World* (New York: Funk and Wagnalls, 1970), 60, in Bard, *Myths and Facts,* 43.

38. Wilson, *Our Father Abraham,* 189.

CHAPTER 9: "ABBA, WHAT'S A CHEESEBURGER?"

1. Noreen S. Ahmed-Ullah, Sam Roe, and Laurie Cohen, "A Rare Look at Secretive Brotherhood in America," *Chicago Tribune,* September 19, 2004, http://www.chicagotribune.com/news/watchdog/chi-0409190261sep19-story.html.

2. Marvin R. Wilson, *Our Father Abraham: Jewish Roots of the Christian Faith* (Grand Rapids: Eerdmans, 1989), 180.

3. Sandra Teplinsky, *Why Still Care About Israel?* (Bloomington, MN: Chosen Books, 2004, 2013), 53.

4. Daniel Juster, face-to-face interview with author, Kansas City, MO, May 20, 2014.

5. Wilson, *Our Father Abraham: Jewish Roots of the Christian Faith,* 168–69.

6. Ibid., 168.

7. Ibid., 185.

8. For more on this topic see, Henri Nouwen, *The Way of the Heart* (New York: Ballantine, 1985) and Benedicta Ward, *The Desert Fathers: Sayings of the Early Christian Monks* (New York: Penguin Putnam Inc., 2003)

9. Juster, interviewed with author.

10. Eric Metaxas, *Bonhoeffer: Pastor, Martyr, Prophet, Spy—A Righteous Gentile vs. the Third Reich* (Nashville: Thomas Nelson, 2010), back flap.

11. "White Rose – Leaflet 4," libcom.org, accessed December 7, 2015, https://libcom.org/library/white-rose-leaflet-4

12. Dietrich Bonhoeffer, *The Cost of Discipleship* (New York: Touchstone, 1959), 43–45.

CHAPTER 10: THE ROAD TO OZ

1. See Charles Taylor, *A Secular Age* (Belknap Press of Harvard University Press, 2007).

2. Christian Smith with Melinda Lundquist Denton, *Soul Searching: The Religious and Spiritual Lives of American Teenagers* (New York: Oxford University Press, 2006), 162–71, 258, 262.

3. Ibid., 162–63.

4. Interview by Michael Cromartie, "What American Teenagers Believe: A Conversation with Christian Smith," *Books & Culture* (January/February 2005): 10, in Michael S. Horton, "Are Churches Secularizing America?" Modern Reformation, accessed July 27, 2015, http://www.modernreformation.org/default.php?page=articledisplay&var2=917.

5. George Barna, *The Second Coming of the Church* (Nashville: Word, 1998), 7.
6. Tim Keller, *Generous Justice: How God's Grace Make Us Just* (New York: Penguin, 2010), 12.
7. Michael Prell, *Underdogma: How America's Enemies Use Our Love for the Underdog to Trash American Power* (Dallas: BenBella Books, 2011), 13.
8. Ibid., 11.
9. Mark Twain, *The Innocents Abroad*, vol. 2, quoted in Caroline Thomas Harnsberger, comp. and ed., *Mark Twain at Your Fingertips: A Book of Quotations*, unabridged repub. (Mineola, NY: Dover, 2009), 347.
10. Jonathan Sacks, *Future Tense: Jews, Judaism, and Israel in the Twenty-First Century* (New York: Random House, 2009), 77.
11. Ibid., 78.
12. "The Final Resolution," *Jewish World* (1908), 189, quoted by "Jewish Quotes," SimpleToRemember.com, accessed August 8, 2015, http://www.simpletoremember.com/articles/a/quotes/.
13. "Jerusalem: Life Throughout the Ages in a Holy City," Bar-Ilan University, accessed July 27, 2015, http://www.biu.ac.il/js/rennert/history_2.html.
14. The modern day equivalents to the nations represented in psalm 83 are as follows: Moab = Central Jordan, Gebal = Lebanon, Ammon = Northern Jordan, Amalek = the Negev desert and Sinai, Philistia = Gaza and Assyria = Syria and Iraq.
15. Sandra Teplinsky, *Why Still Care About Israel?* (Bloomington, MN: Chosen Books, 2004, 2013), 238–39.
16. "Here, then, is the real problem of our negligence. We fail in our duty to study God's Word not so much because it is difficult to understand, not so much because it is dull and boring, but because it is work. Our problem is not a lack of intelligence or a lack of passion. Our problem is that we are lazy." R.C. Sproul, *Knowing Scripture* (Downers Grove, IL: InterVarsity, 1977), 17.
17. Daniel Juster, face-to-face interview with author, Kansas City, MO, May 20, 2014.
18. T. M. Johnson, *Beowulf in Iraq: Lessons from an Ancient Warrior for the Modern Age* (n.p.: Wolf Point: Mjoellnir Ranch/CreateSpace, 2012), 57.
19. Marvin R. Wilson, *Our Father Abraham: Jewish Roots of the Christian Faith* (Grand Rapids: Eerdmans, 1989), 176.
20. Lois Tverberg, "The Wisdom of Hebrew Words," Our Rabbi Jesus, http://ourrabbijesus.com/articles/the-wisdom-of-hebrew-words/.
21. "On Success": Victoria J. Barnett, and Barbara Wojhoski, eds., *Dietrich Bonhoeffer Works, Volume 8: Letters and Papers from Prison* (Minneapolis: Fortress Press, 2010), 42. [October 27, 2015]

APPENDIX 1: CHRISTIAN ANTI-SEMITISM

1. Randy Felton, "Anti-Semitism and the Church," at: http://www.haydid.org/

2. Fritz B. Voll, "A Short Review of a Troubled History," at: http://www.jcrelations.com/ and

3. "Classical and Christian Anti-Semitism," at http://www.virtualjerusalem.co.il/.

4. Fritz B. Voll, "A Short Review of a Troubled History," at: http://www.jcrelations.com/.

5. Max Solbrekken, "The Jews & Jesus: Mistreatment of Jews: Christian shame," at: http://www.mswm.org/

6. Fritz B. Voll, "A Short Review of a Troubled History," at: http://www.jcrelations.com/.

7. "Classical and Christian Anti-Semitism," at: www.virtualjerusalem.co.il/education/

8. "A Calendar of Jewish Persecution," at "HearNow," a Messianic Judaism web site. See: www.hearnow.org/caljp.htm

9. Max Solbrekken, "The Jews & Jesus: Mistreatment of Jews: Christian shame," at: www.mswm.org/jews.htm

10. "Curious and unusual: Rome's ghetto: The old Jewish quarter," at: www.geocities.com/Paris/Arc/5319/roma-c9.html

11. "The Pale of Settlement and the pogroms of 1881 in Russia," at: 204.165.132.2/crucible/whunts/frames_pogromsrussia.htm

12. "The Dreyfus Affair," holocaust.miningco.com/msub15.htm

13. "Protocols of the Elders of Zion," article. See: www.us-israel.org/jsource/anti-semitism/protocols.html

14. Ibid.

15. "Survivors mark Romania pogrom: First memorial to 1941victims," Associated Press, 2000-DEC-6.

16. G.M. Marsden, "Fundamentalism and American Culture,"Oxford University Press, Oxford, UK (1980)

17. G.M. Marsden, "Religion and American Culture,"Harcourt, San Diego, CA, (1990), Page 220.

18. Fritz B. Voll, "A Short Review of a Troubled History," at: www.jcrelations.com/res/incidents.htm#protokols1

19. Robert Fulford, "Historian recalls life as a Jew among the Nazis," Article, Globe and Mail, Toronto ON, 1998-OCT-

20. "A Picture Tells a Thousand Words," www.primenet.com/-rvolk/english/antiprop/jewish_soap/

INDEX

SCRIPTURE INDEX